W. E. Sangster

W. E. Sangster

Sermons in America

A CRITICAL EDITION WITH
INTRODUCTION AND NOTES

Andrew J. Cheatle

WIPF & STOCK · Eugene, Oregon

W. E. SANGSTER
Sermons in America

Wipf & Stock
An Imprint of Wipf and Stock Publishers
199 W. 8th Ave., Suite 3
Eugene, OR 97401

www.wipfandstock.com

PAPERBACK ISBN: 978-1-60899-915-6
HARDCOVER ISBN: 978-1-4982-8527-8
EBOOK ISBN: 978-1-62032-178-2

Manufactured in the U.S.A.

Contents

Preface

THIS BOOK IS THE result of years of research into the life, thought and preaching of W. E. Sangster, my second major writing project on this central figure in mid-twentieth-century world Methodism.

It was through the faith and love of my parents, Lois and Harold Cheatle, that I came to the knowledge of Christ and was brought up listening to sermons every Sunday in the local Nazarene church. Though I'm sure at least some of the sermons must have been good, none have stuck in my memory. So, it was quite a shock that as a young boy, on hearing a vinyl LP in our home of Sangster that I was captivated. Even at that age, I was amazed to hear a preacher whom I could understand, who could hold my attention and have me giggling, and whose sermons I could remember. My mother, already then, a member of the Holiness Movement, was fortunate enough to hear Sangster preach at the Southport Holiness Convention not long after her conversion; the subject being "A Cloud of Witnesses." It is remarkable that a copy of a film made by Arthur Rank, a version of that sermon, is now in my possession. Now that my father has been promoted to glory, I look back to one of my fondest memories with him, which was staying with the Rev. Allan and Eunice Longworth during a trip to London in 1994 to meet Paul Sangster and, of course, being an ex-guard himself, watching the Grenadier Guards practicing "Trooping the Colour." Paul Sangster encouraged my research into his father's legacy, answering important questions during the course of my work and provided me with contacts in order to acquire further taped sermons of his father's preaching. Over and above the collection upon which this book is based, ten other recordings of varying quality capture the clarion voice of Sangster during the 1950s. The materials here presented provide a vital research resource for students of homiletics and Methodism in general, and are a fascinating snapshot in time of one of the twentieth century's greatest preachers. The sermons capture Sangster in his prime, before his favored audience—Methodists, of course—delivering a series of sermons on the subject dearest to his heart: holy living.

Acknowledgments

I AM INDEBTED TO a number of people for their help and support of my research. The Rev. Canon Professor Kenneth Newport and Professor Mary Mills of Liverpool Hope University have through the years provided important mentoring support and have been crucial in guiding me through the many years of research. Professor Newport's decision to accept me as a student when I was much debilitated by a road accident will never be forgotten and changed my life and that of my family positively, and reinforced the lesson to "pay it forward." Indeed, Liverpool Hope University, an ecumenical university where I am privileged to work, has also always supported my research efforts and conference attendance. My colleagues in the Department of Theology, Philosophy and Religious Studies make going to work a joy and delight and are a foretaste of the heavenly family.

My research has required time being spent at the Methodist Archives at the John Rylands Library, Manchester, where I have always been helped and supported by Dr. Gareth Lloyd, with whom I have been fortunate enough to join on a number of collaborative projects at the annual American Academy of Religion sessions in the US, and whose wit and commitment to meticulous scholarship are an inspiration. A special word of appreciation is also due to Professor Dick and Loretta Fish, who supported my research with their generosity and who let us use their apartment for a number of weeks in order for me to acquire dedicated time away from the hustle and bustle of university responsibilities.

My children have always been a source of strength, believing in their "old" dad and his projects, all helping in some way. Daniel Cheatle, our youngest son, helped with some of the initial transcript writing, spending hours trying to crack the code of poor-quality recordings. Anya Cheatle, our daughter-in-law, provided interesting and helpful background information which aided in the annotation, particular tracing Sangster's travel plans. Lisbeth, my Viking wife (and proud of it), has been a constant support, at times aiding me in research, always gladly listening to my chapters, cutting through any sign of pretentiousness and providing invaluable criticisms of language, content and style. Her greatest asset is her dogged determination not to be beaten by SLE Lupus through over thirty years, somehow finding strength to believe in me, encourage and support my efforts—an inspiration to fight on through thick and thin.

My hope is that readers of this book will connect with the passion behind the project in all its facets and that Sangster's voice, now silent, will be heard once more through these sermons.

Abbreviations

CHPCM   Franz Hildebrandt and Oliver A. Beckerlegge, editors, *A Collection of Hymns for the Use of the People Called Methodist*, vol. 7 of *The Works of John Wesley*, Bicentennial Edition (Nashville: Abingdon, 1983)

ODNB   *Oxford Dictionary of National Biography*, online ed. (Oxford: Oxford University Press, 2004)

INTRODUCTION

W. E. Sangster: Methodist Preacher

PERHAPS NO TWENTIETH-CENTURY METHODIST preacher was as well known on both sides of the Atlantic during their lifetime as William Edwin Robert Sangster (1900–60), a figure of formidable reputation and respect. His life story and contribution as a Methodist theologian have been rehearsed elsewhere in print, and as vital as these sources are in providing a more comprehensive framework for understanding Sangster's contribution to Methodism and British church life, this study seeks to contribute to understanding him as a preacher.[1]

During his life Sangster was one of the few British preachers who could attract crowds wherever he went. Not only was he a preacher of immense standing but he was also a prolific student and author of homiletics, writing five books on various aspects of preaching and publishing numerous books of his own sermons. His standing as a preacher is illustrated by the fact that he was emulated by scores of young British preachers, some of whom not only followed his style but also went so far as to mimic his accent. His books of sermons and preaching were reprinted numerous times on both sides of the Atlantic.

In my previous engagement with Sangster's work, which took a particularly theological approach, I concluded that he should be viewed as a major Wesleyan theologian, attempting to restate key Methodist doctrines in the twentieth-century world, following a form of demythologising programme. Sangster still sits at the forefront of Methodist scholarship in attempting to wrestle with the gap between the world of the Wesleys and the nuclear world. For Sangster, however, this theological task was always seen within the larger

---

1. The most comprehensive biography of Sangster was written by his son, Paul Sangster, *Doctor Sangster*. Simon Ross Valentine's book *William Edwin Sangster* follows for the most part Paul Sangster's lead. Andrew J. Cheatle's *W. E. Sangster – Herald of Holiness* and *William Sangster: Heir of John Wesley?* offer a more critical biographical survey and theological engagement with Sangster's thought.

picture of preaching the kerygma; the preaching event was always in view. Few in the history of Methodism, if any, have written or spoken as much as him about the Wesleyan doctrines of sanctification and perfection, publishing three books on the subject, and scores of articles, pamphlets and sermons. Yet, here in this book we have Sangster's homiletical engagement with this aspect of his Methodist inheritance.

This present work focuses, therefore, on the preaching of W. E. Sangster and makes a unique contribution to scholarship within two fields: Wesleyan/Methodist history, and homiletics. This new venture brings into the public domain ten sermons delivered by Sangster on the occasion of the 1956 World Methodist Conference in Junaluska, North Carolina. These lengthy sermons have all of been transcribed accurately from recordings. Nine of the sermons are previously unpublished in this form. One sermon, entitled "Called to Be Saints," was published in the *Proceedings* of the conference, but heavily edited.[2] The version in this collection is true to what Sangster actually said, being transcribed directly from recordings. Six of the sermons were preached sequentially on the subject of holy living. According to Sangster's own words this was the first time he had spoken on holiness sequentially. A little over a year after these sermons were delivered he began to feel the effects of the disease that would eventually kill him and he would never repeat the series. This series of sermons on aspects of Christian holiness would therefore be the only time he preached this way. So, this book places before the reader some of Sangster's most mature thought on holiness and its application in daily life, and the first and last sequential series Sangster preached on the subject.

Methodology

With regard to homiletics and preaching, this book features ten sermons transcribed directly from recordings. Sangster's extant published sermons were highly polished and made for reading, and bore only a remote resemblance to their oral delivery. The transcripts in this collection are, in contrast, true to what was actually spoken, and as much as possible reflect how it was said. Little attention has been placed, therefore, to the fineries of literary style or grammatical correctness, but rather closeness to the original utterance. Sangster often started sentences with the conjunctions *but* and *and*, which abound, as does his customary "My dear friends." Typical of his oratory was parenthetical speech; starting a thought, interrupting it briefly and returning,

2. Clark and Perkins, eds., *Proceedings of the Ninth World Methodist Conference*, 358–65.

sometimes in mid-sentence, sometimes a few sentences later.[3] I have endeavoured as much as possible to commit to print what was spoken, even though at times some words and phrases were not entirely clear and were notoriously difficult to follow on the tapes, due to the poor recording quality and aging. I have also retained words, phrases and idioms from Sangster's mid-twentieth-century British English parle, derived as they were from a particular historical context. Some of his language now seems odd and outdated, with some words having changed meaning subsequently, some becoming politically incorrect and some even unacceptable or bordering on the offensive in today's world. The same could also be said of Sangster's sometimes paternal point of view, both being arguably a remnant of British Methodism being perceived as the "mother church" of Methodism but perhaps also a vestige of notions of empire, for only recently in his lifetime had the British Empire begun to enter its death throes. Therefore quotations, where given, are in the words and style of the authors concerned and no responsibility for non-inclusive language and ideas rests with me. I understood my task as transcriber to be historically accurate rather than to modify for contemporary conventions and values. It is hoped by this process that students of homiletics will now be able to compare the two forms of the sermon: the *literary form* from his published sermons and, as a result of this study, the *spoken* or *oral form*. A suggested and convenient starting point for such a comparative study would be the two versions of "Called to Be Saints" previously mentioned, though it has not been possible to substantiate unequivocally whether Sangster was responsible for the editing of the version published in the 1956 *World Methodist Proceedings*.

The original source(s) of the recordings is shrouded in mystery. Even the World Methodist Council, museum and archives do not seem to know how and by whom these sermons were recorded. What we do know is that ten of Sangster's sermons from the time of the 1956 World Methodist Conference were recorded, probably on reel tape, which was the technology in use at the time.[4] These, it would appear, were copied individually decades later and appeared randomly on cassette tapes and never circulated as a collection. In the 1980s, as I began to collect tapes, books, articles and letters of Sangster, I was able gradually to reconstruct the 1956 series by a combination of painstaking research and "providence."[5]

3. Indicated in the transcripts by an em dash (—).

4. It seems that one to two more sermons were delivered as part of the series on holiness, probably focusing on prayer. This is evident from Sangster's introduction to the sermon entitled "Guidance."

5. One example of which was my parents sitting in a café in Morecombe, England and speaking of my research, and an elderly gentleman, overhearing and joining in their conversation about Sangster, said, "Oh, I have some tapes of Sangster." From this

Sangster in the US

The sermons in this unique collection re-emphasise the long-held view of older students of homiletics and preaching that William Sangster was a preacher of immense ability and power. Yet few people today are actually familiar with his large collection of written sermons or his extensive writings on homiletics.[6] The taped sermons of Sangster which form the raw material of the transcripts within this book are crafted examples of scholarly preaching and communicative brilliance which any contemporary devotee of preaching or student of homiletics should be obliged to listen to and to study.[7]

Sangster's preaching made him a nationally and internationally recognised figure, even grabbing numerous newspaper headlines in January 1953 for his sermon "Sermon for Britain," which detailed what a revival of the Christian religion would do for Britain. His renown translated into popularity in the US too, something of a rarity then for an Englishman, pre-TV and Internet, with many of his books being published under American titles. At the height of Dr. Billy Graham's fame, Paul Sangster says that Dr. Graham introduced Sangster to the Camp Meeting at Junaluska, North Carolina, where these recordings took place, as "a preacher without peer in the world."[8] Though it has not been unequivocally possible to document the veracity of Paul Sangster's claim, Dr. Graham's office indicates the high esteem Graham had for Sangster as a preacher:

> It would be like looking for a "needle in a haystack" to be able to document that "preacher without peer in the world" quote since I would really need to know the year it might have been written in a letter, and to whom. Of course, it might just have been a verbal comment. So I cannot confirm those exact words, I am afraid. I did ask Mr. Graham about Dr. Sangster, though, and he did indeed think a lot of his preaching. He said he loved him, and that he had been a guest in their home. I am sorry that I do not know when that was, although I assume it might have been sometime when Dr. Sangster was at Lake Junaluska.[9]

I acquired four of the taped sermons. See Cheatle, "Reflections on the Creation of a Research Archive."

6. See the bibliography. His best-known book on homiletics was *Craft of the Sermon* (1954), which was a combination volume of *The Craft of Sermon Illustration* (1946) and *The Craft of Sermon Construction* (1949).

7. An online audio archive is being developed at Liverpool Hope University, which will make a number of the better quality recordings available for research purposes.

8. P. Sangster, *Doctor Sangster*, 265.

9. Private email to the author, March 13, 2012.

Sangster was, for his times, quite a regular visitor to the US, gaining through the years a high regard in the American churches. His first recorded visit was in 1938, sailing to New York as the British representative at the Conference of the United Church of Canada in the October of that year. His stay included time in New York, where, according to his son, he was struck by the skyscrapers of Manhattan, before moving to Toronto and Ottawa for the conference, about which Sangster reported in the *Methodist Recorder*.[10]

The dangers of travelling in the war years, plus his added responsibilities for the Westminster Air shelter during WWII, prevented his return to the US until 1947, when he sailed on the newly overhauled and refurbished RMS Mauretania for the occasion of the Methodist Ecumenical Conference at Springfield, Massachusetts. The travelling party to the conference included other notable Methodists, such as Eric Baker and E. Benson Perkins. Before the responsibilities of conference attendance Sangster visited Washington, D.C., preaching on September 14 at two consecutive morning services at Mount Vernon Place United Methodist Church and the evening service at Foundry United Methodist Church.[11] On Friday September 19 he preached at Asbury United Methodist Church, before moving on to Baltimore to preach on the subject of grace at the Sunday morning service at the historically significant Lovely Lane Methodist Church, the "mother church of American Methodism."[12] His final preaching engagement before the conference took place at Mount Vernon Place United Methodist Church and Asbury House, Baltimore. On the following Wednesday Sangster visited Trinity United Methodist Church in Springfield, Massachusetts, followed by the conference itself at the Municipal Auditorium for the ecumenical conference, about which he wrote an extended article in the *Methodist Recorder,* which gives real insight into the concerns of everyday Americans about the threat of communism and atomic war.[13]

Only a few months later at the start of 1948 Sangster flew for the first time to the US via Iceland and Montreal before arriving by train in New York. His first official visit was at Mount Vernon United Methodist Church, Danville, Virginia, just catching the final days of the Rev. Dr. Edward Rees's

10. *Methodist Recorder*, October 27, 1938, 9.

11. While the United Methodist Church was not formed until 1968 when the Methodist Church and the Evangelical United Brethren Church merged, they are being referred to in this way for the benefit of the modern reader.

12. Formally known as First Methodist Episcopal Church, Baltimore. The original Lovely Lane Chapel was the location of the 1784 "Christmas Conference," at which the US Methodist Church was founded and at which Francis Asbury and Thomas Coke were ordained as its first bishops.

13. *Methodist Recorder*, October 9, 1947, 6; and P. Sangster, *Doctor Sangster*, 246.

ministry.[14] The main purpose of his visit was to give the Sam Jones Lectures on Evangelism at Emory University, Atlanta, Georgia, where he arrived on January 17 after a short stop-off at Duke University, Durham, North Carolina. His lectures were later published as *Let Me Commend*. Sangster's journal gives his own thoughts about the lecture series:

> I think I had some hesitation when I was on the way about the wisdom of coming: whether, indeed, it was worth the time and expense, and being away from home and Westminster; or whether *anything* I could say justified the trouble and effort of it. I don't feel that now. It seems a wonderful opportunity to have had, and an experience unique in my ministry. It was like addressing the Methodist Conference day after day for a week, with no business to intrude but only the business of advancing the Kingdom by evangelism.
>
> Have I taken it well? Only God knows—but I have truly tried. Both in the preparation and delivery I did my best. Discounting, as I will, most of what these dear, exuberant fellows say of my help to them, I feel, in other ways, that God took over the whole thing and used me. I am certain many, many men have a new and higher idea of their office, and many have gone back to do the work of the Evangelist. The ministry of the lectures will be continued, I trust, in their publication, and the men reminded of the things I said. Those who were not there will get the substance of it, if they wish, that way, and perhaps on both sides of the Atlantic their effect may be felt. It is not my disposition to exaggerate, I think, the value of the unimportant things I do, but, on the other hand, I have no mind to belittle the work of God, nor His condescending use of me.[15]

The rest of the visit included preaching at a number of local churches and attending official banquets, one including that of the state governor, and an absolute highlight was getting to know the eccentric tycoon and founder of the Coca-Cola company Asa Griggs Candler, after whom the Department of Divinity was named at Emory University.[16]

It would be over six years before Sangster would return to the States; the culmination of his 1954 world tour, arriving on July 14 in Los Angeles.[17]

14. "History of Mount Vernon United Methodist Church: Our Seventh Decade (1944–1954)," http://mtvernonumc.org/History%20of%20Mt%20Vernon-7th%20decade.htm.

15. Quoted from Sangster's personal journal by his son, Paul Sangster, in *Doctor Sangster*, 249–50.

16. P. Sangster, *Doctor Sangster*, 250–51.

17. He had previously sailed to India, later visiting churches in Sri Lanka, Australia, New Zealand and Fiji. A detailed log of his enterprise was sent on a regular basis to the

His principal engagements were in Ocean City and Lake Junaluska, though he preached at services in Los Angeles, San Diego, Pasadena, Chicago, and Philadelphia.

Ralph Luff of Ocean City Tabernacle was arguably the instigator of Sangster's 1954 appearance in the US. According to William G. Luff, "armed with a letter of introduction from Bishop Corson," Ralph Luff made a dedicated journey to London in the spring of 1953 to secure Sangster's services for the summer of 1954 for a major anniversary of the Ocean City Tabernacle. William Luff says:

> Explaining that it was our 75th Anniversary and that we were going to celebrate a Special Year, Ralph Luff emphasised that we wanted to celebrate this "special year" around Dr. Sangster. Dr. Sangster was already a world-renowned preacher. He was the Minister of the great Central Hall in London, who Sunday after Sunday preached to congregations exceeding 3000 people. At the time he was the most listened-to preacher on national radio in the British Empire, reaching an audience into the hundreds of thousands.
>
> Ralph Luff felt good on the air flight coming back from England. He had received Dr. Sangster's commitment to come to America in 1954 to be the anchor of a great array of preachers to be heard by the Tabernacle congregations.[18]

At Lake Junaluska he spoke at morning and evening services for five days to a large audiences of around two thousand people.[19] It was also at Junaluska he became acquainted with Billy Graham for the first time.

Sangster returned to the US in late July 1956 primarily to attend the World Methodist Conference, though his schedule was quite punishing. Between his arrival and mid-September he travelled to Ocean City to participate in a series of services at the Tabernacle before being the main speaker at the Camp Meetings at Lake Junaluska, which was followed by his attendance at the World Methodist Conference itself. According to Sangster's own notes he drove to New York on August 16, before his broadcast at the Columbia Broadcasting Corporation on Sunday August 19.[20]

At Lake Junaluska Sangster was preceded in the pulpit by Billy Graham, who left shortly before Sangster arrived, and who promised the audience "a preacher without peer in the world."[21] On route home he was conferred a

Methodist Recorder.

18. Luff, *Story of the Ocean City Tabernacle*, 66.

19. P. Sangster, *Doctor Sangster*, 261–63.

20. P. Sangster, *Doctor Sangster*, 261–63.

21. See previous discussion of this statement.

LL.D. degree by Southern Methodist University, met President Eisenhower and visited the grave of Francis Asbury at Mount Olivet Cemetery, Baltimore, Maryland.

Altogether on this occasion Sangster was in the US for close to nine weeks. Over and above his preaching and speaking he authored two more pamphlets from the Westminster Pamphlets series and had an article published in the *Reader's Digest*, returning home on the luxury liner RMS Queen Mary.

Sangster's final visit to the US was in January 1958, flying into Dallas, Texas, to deliver lectures on preaching at Southern Methodist University, later published under the title *Power in Preaching*.[22] At the start of the lectures Sangster felt that the audience were unresponsive and did not understand his humor, perhaps not helped by the effects of his illness on his voice, which had become much affected during 1958; something that is clearly evident from the recording of Sangster's preaching at the Cliff College, Derbyshire, on Pentecost weekend a few months later, where his tone is lower and his pace of speech is much slower and the pronunciation slurred.[23]

It could be argued that 1950–56 were the zenith years of Sangster's preaching ministry, reaching millions through books and camp meetings and the media. Little did he or his audiences know that his voice would soon be stilled by illness. Following his death in May 1960 *The Methodist Recorder* and numerous British newspapers carried tributes to his life and ministry and legacy, all paying homage to his preaching, some even designating him "the prince of preachers."[24]

Sangster the Preacher

The tapes utilised within this book belong to a collection of recordings of Sangster in the possession of the author, all from the time period 1950–58. These are a remarkable collection of taped sermons delivered on key important occasions, the largest discreet collection being the ones utilised in this study. These recordings allow the reader to encounter Sangster in the raw, so to speak, flowing at his best, a tribute to the abundance of preaching talent in mid-twentieth-century British Methodism.

Sangster's influence on preaching is still acknowledged nearly sixty years since his death. Homileticians like Carol M. Noren comment on Sangster's

22. W. E. Sangster, *Power in Preaching*.

23. P. Sangster, *Doctor Sangster*, 266–67.

24. *Methodist Recorder*, June 2, 1962, 4.

style and influence as a preacher. "It isn't easy to say how much the ethos of British Methodism shaped W. E. Sangster and how much he shaped it. Suffice it to say that his sermons exemplify the best of that strand of homiletics in the 20th century." Noren contends that Sangster's homiletical method still has much to offer the church in the postmodern era. "The timely references in his messages may date him, yet aspects of his method provide a model for preaching in the post-modern world: knowing the world of the listener, taking the listener's experience seriously, and embodying the hope we have in Christ."[25] Indeed, added to these points must be his rich use of illustration from everyday life situations combined with his ability of storytelling with drama and empathetic emotion, clearly evident in these sermons. David L. Larsen further supports this view. "Sangster's short introductions and conclusions, saving sense of humor and emotional intensity (he was always dramatic) gave thrust and entre into human hearts in need."[26]

Sangster's great skill, demonstrated often dramatically in the following sermons, was telling stories in order to illuminate biblical and theological truths. Larsen considered him to be "a master at illustration. . . . His work on sources and variety of illustration and the dangerous illustration are most helpful, and his practical suggestions on gleaning illustrations from our reading are trenchant and relevant."[27] Tom Long credits Sangster in influencing the inductive method of one of America's most influential preachers and homiletians: Fred Craddock.[28]

Sangster's preached sermons also anticipated much of the last twenty years of narrative preaching, albeit sticking close to the centralities of the Christian faith, something that many practitioners have been guilty of forgetting. It would be doubtful to hear Sangster preaching on anything but the risen Christ on Easter Sunday morning, rather than amorphous references to the human need to hug trees and embrace wildlife, sometimes heard in Methodist churches today on this most important day in the church's calender.[29]

Though acknowledged by the vast majority of preachers as a giant of preaching, not all of Sangster's contemporaries, however, were enamoured with his style and method. Indeed, during Sangster's lifetime it was suspected that Dr. Martyn Lloyd-Jones, geographically just down the road from

25. Noren, "Ten Greatest Preachers of the Twentieth Century," 8.

26. Larsen, "William E. Sangster: In the Wake of the Wesleys."

27. Larsen, "William E. Sangster: In the Wake of the Wesleys."

28. From a personal interview at Emory University in November 2010 and email correspondence.

29. An application derived from the Easter story heard by the author recently at a Methodist church.

Westminster Central Hall, was not altogether an admirer. Austin B. Tucker has recently revealed a letter he received from Lloyd-Jones in 1965 concerning Sangster's preaching:

> When I was a seminary student, I wrote to D. Lloyd-Jones of Westminster Chapel, London, to ask his opinion on the use of sermon illustrations. He responded graciously with a note about his "strong views on the subject." He reminded me that he had always been a critic of a man like W. E. Sangster, who used to carry a little notebook in his pocket to take down any stories he heard and who had a "card-index of illustrations appropriate to various subjects." Lloyd-Jones said, "I always described that as the prostitution of preaching!"[30]

Lloyd-Jones's tirade against Sangster didn't stop there. Six years later, while attacking the importance of "homiletics" in general, Lloyd-Jones launched into him again, this time in print. "Lastly, and only lastly, Homiletics. This is to me an abomination," says Lloyd Jones. He continues, "There are books bearing such titles as *The Craft of Sermon Construction*, and *The Craft of Sermon Illustration*. That is, to me, prostitution. Homiletics just comes in, but no more."[31] Combining his staunchly defended Reformed position on the primacy of Scripture with his utter distaste for Sangster's homiletical method, it would surely have disappointed Lloyd-Jones therefore that a ThD was awarded for a study of Sangster's preaching at a well-known Baptist seminary in 1968.[32] The ultimate horror would surely be, however, that the young Baptist who received his toxic letter about Sangster in 1965 would forty-three years later write a book which essentially propagates Sangster's method and practice. Indeed, with a little modernising, Tucker includes the absolute importance of collecting stories and illustrations in his chapter entitled "An Endless Supply of Stories," a practice despised by Lloyd-Jones, but fundamentally a part of Sangster's method.[33] Though having written a number of books on homiletics, perhaps Sangster's cautionary note about "the art of preaching" in a little-known book would have brought these two preachers closer to a common understanding:

> Preaching? Yes! But not preaching as a fine art; not stylistic, essay-like compositions pleasing to "men of taste," polished and half-unconsciously aiming to provoke admiration for the author.

30. Tucker, *Preacher as Storyteller*, 20.

31. D. Lloyd-Jones, *Preaching and Preachers*, 118–19.

32. Dorr, "Critique of the Preaching of William Edwin Robert Sangster."

33. Tucker, *Preacher as Storyteller*, 127–39.

But elemental preaching, with a sense of "givenness" all over it, drenched in prayer, clearly out to do something, challenging, all but dragging men into the presence of God and shaking "the trembling gates of hell."[34]

It appears therefore that time has vindicated Sangster's method and practice of preaching, which included the importance of illustration and compelling storytelling, which are clearly being reevaluated, prised and copied today, though the motivation and goal are the clear pronouncement of the gospel, not showiness or self-glorification.

As regards Sangster's place in the history of preaching, Larsen goes so far as to say, "Sangster was unquestionably part of the royalty of the pulpit in the last century; and though long silenced, we would profit by reading him. [He] may well be, more than we realise, something of a man for our times as well."[35] It is hoped that this volume of "spoken sermons" will only add to that legacy.

The Content of His Preaching

Sangster's sermons generally stick close to the application of the gospel to everyday life. Rarely did Sangster preach expository sermons or long complexly argued sermons on theological doctrines with doctrine as the focus. This has led Sangster, along with the whole of mid-twentieth-century Methodism, to be open to the criticism that their theology was lacking in theological substance. D. Martyn Lloyd-Jones, himself a dedicated expositional preacher, identified such a lack due to the Arminian roots of Methodism, which tended, according to him, to focus on more pastoral and practical issues. "Arminianism," he said, "is ultimately, non-theological."[36] Iain Murray picks up the point further, attributing the malaise to John Wesley, for according to him, John Wesley "was a great evangelist but no theologian." Murray further hypothesises that the decline of Methodism in Britain in the twentieth century was because it inherited its lack of theology from its founder.[37]

---

34. W. E. Sangster, "Richmond and Evangelism," 25–26.

35. Larsen, "William E. Sangster: In the Wake of the Wesleys."

36. D. Martyn Lloyd-Jones, *Preaching and Preachers*, 101.

37. Murray, *Wesley and the Men Who Followed*, 249–63. The general thrust of the criticisms fails to recognise that Arminius was no mean theologian—actually a Calvinist himself—and demonstrates a rather limited acquaintance with the huge theological corpus within the writings of John and Charles Wesley, and further fails to appreciate that the Wesleys were already working within a historical, ecclesial and theological environment within the Church of England, presupposing a heritage on most points which needed little discussion.

Whatever the truth or falsity of such charges, particularly in reference to the twentieth century, the evidence of Sangster's written sermons and the sermons utilised within this book closely follow his strong key belief that preaching must be rooted in sound Christian doctrine. Correspondingly, he was adamant about the importance of doctrinal preaching. The subject matter of sermons derived from his view of the essential nature of the Christian faith.[38] "Christianity," according to Sangster, "is not vague sentiment or an amiable feeling."[39] Typical of Sangster's more colourful use of language, he says, "It is not 'being kind to grandmother and the cat.'"[40] According to Sangster the Christian faith is a hard, dogmatic core of doctrine that centres on a living Person, built on certain historical facts concerning Christ with a number of, what he calls, "immense affirmations regarding God, man and the universe."[41] No less a figure than Horton Davies in his landmark book *The Varieties of English Preaching 1900–1960* confirmed Sangster's commitment to sound theological content in his preaching. "Dr. W. E. Sangster excelled in doctrinal preaching."[42] The sermons in this collection represent one particular area of Christian theology, namely soteriology, and illustrate in particular his practical engagement with the Methodist emphasis of sanctification within the broader framework of holy living.

Understanding and Experiencing Holiness

When the sermons which form this collection were preached in 1956, Sangster had become engaged in more interdenominational relations, especially during his time as Secretary of Home Missions (1955–58) within the British Methodist Church. It is during this time that subtle changes in theological emphasis became apparent in his thinking, evidenced by the use of more "catholic" or ecumenical language.

At work here is the post-WWII context of interchurch dialogue in Britain, his own interdenominational activity and his attempts to bring unity within British Methodism. The Second World War and its consequences had led questions being asked in Britain about the continued validity of denominationalism. In 1946 Archbishop Geoffrey Fisher's famous Cambridge sermon created an atmosphere of dialogue between denominations about future possibilities of

38. W. E. Sangster, *Doctrinal Preaching*, 4–5.
39. W. E. Sangster, *Doctrinal Preaching*, 4–5.
40. W. E. Sangster, *Doctrinal Preaching*, 7.
41. W. E. Sangster, *Power in Preaching*, 34–35.
42. Davies, *Varieties of English Preaching*, 197.

union. Preached at Great St. Mary's Cambridge on November 23, 1946, Fisher's sermon entitled "A Step Forward in Church Relations" proposed that churches work creatively toward establishing full communion.[43]

Sangster was also affected by the spirit of this time, throwing himself into large scale evangelistic programmes, both Methodist and particularly interdenominational. Also in the year prior to the World Methodist Conference in 1956, and afterwards, Sangster was engaged in attempts to negotiate unity within his own denomination seeking a common consensus between the two evangelical poles within British Methodism for the sake of cooperation in evangelism.[44] So, the period 1946–56 saw Sangster seeking to place what he saw as the essence of Methodist thinking within a broader ecclesial framework.

This more ecumenical ethos was also apparent in Sangster's continuing engagement with the Methodist emphasis on holiness, his particular passion, which continued unabated in this period. *The Pure in Heart* (1954) demonstrates a remarkable ecumenical approach to holiness while still seeking to maintain a particular Methodist position. In this book Sangster investigated the quest for holiness and the perceptions of saintliness across denominational boundaries, evidencing a particular interest in the Spanish sixteenth-century mystics.

Excerpts from the unique series of sermons within this collection were later printed in the Westminster Pamphlet series, under the titles *You Can Be a Saint* (1957), *How to Live in Christ* (1957), and *How Much Are You Saved?* (1959).[45] Subsequently Sangster edited and published larger extracts from the sermons in this volume in his practical book on holy living, *The Secret of Radiant Life* (1957), though in a much-changed order. These sermons, therefore, demonstrate Sangster's later thinking on holy living. His emphasis was that the holy life is liveable in the real world and is open to all, not just monastics. The techniques of saints from the long history of the church can and should be utilised in everyday life. The sermons are therefore immensely practical, rather than theoretical.

In the two years before his death, when his own physical efforts were waning due to his illness, the focus of his continuing writings on holy living was on the value of prayer and contemplation, in order to prepare the church for future revival; his thoughts being published in the *Joyful News* and especially in the *Prayer Cell Messenger*.

43. Fisher, "Archbishop Fisher's Cambridge Sermon, 1946," 441, n4.

44. See, for example, W. E. Sangster, "Bible Basis for All That We Believe," 3.

45. W. E. Sangster, *You Can Be a Saint*; *How to Live in Christ*; and *How Much Are You Saved?*

Altogether, therefore Sangster's study of sanctity and his published outputs on the Methodist understanding of holiness had continued for over twenty years before this present series of sermons, originally beginning around 1936.[46] His first published efforts were printed in the *Methodist Recorder* and later brought together in *Methodism Can Be Born Again* (1938), which were written to bring attention to the state of Methodism two hundred years after John Wesley's Aldersgate experience. His first writings on holiness were primarily devotional and can be readily aligned, broadly speaking, with a conservative evangelical point of view, though Sangster raised some concerns about the continued validity of John Wesley's concept of sin, feeling it was too weak.

Sangster's best-known writings on holiness, however, were his two major studies of Christian sanctity: *The Path to Perfection* (1943), which primarily focused on the Methodist legacy of holiness from John Wesley, and the aforementioned *The Pure in Heart* (1954). Both books are significant indicators of some major repositioning in his understanding of Christian holiness. His 1943 book, which was the fruit of his PhD studies, approached the Methodist understanding of holiness through the methods and language of modern theological study. His ultimate aim was to construct or restate the Methodist understanding of holiness for the twentieth-century context, therefore presupposing the acceptance of modern science and study, including humankind's evolutionary beginnings, the importance and use of historical critical method, and the application of psychological paradigms in order to better understand the human condition, with a particular openness to its Jungian branch.[47] Within the British context Sangster's theological position in these years would have been best described as a guarded liberal evangelicalism, but one that rarely deviated from a centrist position on fundamental doctrines. His approach was firmly rejected, however, by the leaders of the British Holiness Movement, who felt that he was betraying the Wesleyan doctrine of holiness as stated by John Wesley.[48]

Between these two major works on holiness Sangster wrote a multitude of articles on the subject, especially during his presidential year of 1950–51. His presidential address focused on the Methodist heritage of holiness, which was followed with a major series in the *Methodist Recorder*. His

46. For a full discussion of Sangster's engagement with the Methodist doctrines of sanctification and perfection, see my book, Cheatle, *W. E. Sangster – Herald of Holiness*, and my published lecture, Cheatle, *William Sangster: Heir of John Wesley?*

47. The first evidence of his changing viewpoint can be found in *These Things Abide* (1939).

48. James, "Dr. Sangster's New Book."

"Sermon for Britain," part of his large contribution to the 1953 Methodist Year of Evangelism, continued his engagement with the themes of holiness but evidences a clear movement towards a more corporate and social understanding of holiness.

All in all, in the twenty-year period prior to the preaching of this collection of sermons in Junaluska, and following it until his death in May 1960, Sangster had been the clarion voice calling for Methodism's theological, existential and social engagement with John Wesley's doctrine of Christian holiness.

These sermons are, therefore, a major resource in understanding how this highly influential British theologian and preacher sought to earth all the years of his research and engagement with the Methodist concern and passion for holiness into a series of sermons delivered to an international Methodist audience at this most important conference. As such, it could be said these are the final systematic spoken words of William Edwin Sangster on the subject of holiness.

CHAPTER 1

Unconditional Surrender

THE WORD *IF* IS a very little word but, by common consent, a most important word. It labels the hypothetical. No important categorical statement
ever began with the word *if*. A big *perhaps* overhangs every assertion that
begins this way. "If President Eisenhower were to fall ill again."[1] "If the Suez
Canal was cut."[2] "If a great world revival broke out as a result of our World
Methodist Conference."[3]

"*If!*"

My friends, I have two biblical *ifs* for you this evening: "If God will be
with me and keep me in the way that I go, and will give me bread to eat and
raiment to put on, then shall the Lord be my God" [Gen 28:20–21]. "Our God,
whom we serve is able to deliver us from the burning fiery furnace, but if not,
we will not serve thy Gods nor worship the golden image thou hast set up"
[Dan 3:17–18]. Let us glance at those texts in turn, and I need hardly tell you
I have a spiritual purpose in all this.

Jacob loved a bargain! Oh he loved it! "Oh yes," you say, "of course he did;
he was a Jew!" Most Gentiles, I know, love a bargain too. The peculiarity with

1. Sangster is probably referring to President Eisenhower's heart attack of Autumn
1955, whose health was much debated during the presidential campaign of 1956. For a
detailed discussion of the political interpretations of Eisenhower's 1955 medical situation,
see Gilbert, "Eisenhower's 1955 Heart Attack."

2. Just prior to the World Methodist Conference in 1956, Egyptian president Gamal
Abdel Nasser had announced the nationalisation of the Suez Canal Company (July 26,
1956), antagonising the British and French governments, who had owned and operated
the Suez Canal since its construction in 1869. Only three months later a full-blown crisis
developed that threatened world peace, when Israel invaded the Sinai Peninsula and British and French troops occupied the Canal zone. See Brown, "1956: Suez and the End of
Empire."

3. The ninth World Methodist Conference was held in Lake Junaluska, North Carolina
in August–September 1956.

Jacob was this: that he carried over his bargaining into his dealings with the Almighty. He didn't only like a bargain when he could get it between man and man, but he could love a bargain when it was made between man and God. He said so, to God himself. He thought, "When you make a bargain"—it was a very good thing, said Jacob—"have it clear. Have it clear both ways." "You're committed to this, to all of it, and I'm committed to this." "Now, if God will be with me, and will keep me in the ways that I go, and will give me bread to eat and raiment to put on, and bring me in safety to my father's house, then shall the Lord be my God." He was willing to be a servant, on conditions. He was ready to take a vow if it was quite clear what God was committed to as well. "*If* God will be with me, *then!*"

Contrast that with the mental state of these three brave boys. They were what we would call today displaced persons. They were living in a country not their own. They were conforming with the rules of that country in everything that was not incompatible with their conscience. There was just one area of their life where they couldn't conform. They couldn't go back on their God. They would have nothing to do with idolatry. So, they were facing this awful alternative. They had either to bow down and worship the golden image or to be cast into the midst of the burning fiery furnace. They didn't hesitate. They said, "Our God whom we serve is able to deliver us from the burning fiery furnace." They didn't doubt his capacity to do it. He could do it! What they weren't sure about was this: whether he would do it!

Sometimes God allows his servants to pass out of sight of men unvindicated. They didn't know if he would. They knew he could! They didn't know if he would. But that wasn't going to make any difference, if he didn't. If he didn't. If he allowed them to pass through the burning fiery furnace, and perish in it, "even so we will not bow down to the golden image thou hast set up."

My friends, with those two *ifs* before us, with that contrasted state of mind clearly fixed in our thinking now, I want, I want, to begin by making two or three important assertions which it seems it would be good for us to have clear in our mind at the beginning of our week.

You are Christian people. I believe it. Only Christian people would be spending their holiday this way. You want to get deeper into religion. I am sure that far the majority of you, maybe all of you, have said yes to God. In your hearts you are disciples. But your great [need], even mine, is to get still deeper into our most holy faith. And there are impediments in us to that deeper discipleship. And some of those impediments we are not fully aware ourselves.[4]

---

4. For a discussion of Sangster's understanding of sin and the unconscious see Cheatle, *William Sangster: Herald of Holiness*, 110–13.

Let me point them out to you on the background of these two *ifs*, the *if* that bargains and the *if* that asks no questions at all.

And I begin by saying: never make conditions with God! Never! Never make conditions with God. Conditions do not live from earth to heaven. Oh, but you say, "God makes conditions with us!"

Of course! Of course!

Because he is God! He can!

The Bible is full of his glorious conditions. Conditions live from heaven to earth, but not from earth to heaven. Listen to some of the conditional promises of God. He said:

> "If you will return unto me, then I will return unto you" [Mal 3:7].

> "If you will bring the whole tithe to the storehouse, then I will open the windows of heaven and pour you out a blessing" [Mal 3:10].

> "If you will walk in the light as he is in the light, then the blood of Jesus Christ will cleanse you from all sin" [1 John 1:7].

Oh yes. They are just a handful of God's conditions to us. He loves so to address us. He says, "If you will do this, I will do that."

I am saying to you this evening, it isn't mete that we reverse that process. It isn't for us to go to God as Jacob did and say, "Now look, look, if you do this, and this, and this, and this, then I'll belong to you. Oh really, and I'll give a tenth as well. How generous I am. I will, if you'll do all that." It is not mete.

The meek state of any mortal in relation to his God is one of *unconditional surrender*. "Nothing in my hands I bring, simply to thy cross I cling."[5]

I'm asking you as I begin; I'm asking myself the question, "Are you living in that state of unconditional surrender?" "Are you the meek state of mortals," I repeat myself, "with their God, with the state of unconditional surrender"?

I can be intimate with you, my dear friends. I'm intimate; I'm helping you this week and we're old friends now. I'm going to say this to you intimately: that I've found in my own spiritual life that whenever I've started making conditions with God I was falling back from full surrender. Whenever I started slipping what I will call "parentheses" into my prayers—"I'll do anything for you Lord, except this"—the moment, the moment there were parentheses in my prayers, I was losing spiritual tone. I was falling back. I was not, in the very nature of things, a completely committed man.

Years ago in the city of York, after which your New York is named, which you don't need to be reminded—one of the few place names in America that I

---

5. Quoted from the first two lines of the third stanza of Augustus M. Toplady's (1740–78) well-known hymn "Rock of Ages Cleft for Me."

can't parallel in England is Junaluska, and you can have that—years ago I knelt down in the city of York and the fathers of the church placed their hands on my head, and I was ordained to this holy ministry. And I took vows and I said that I would obey those placed in authority over me. And I would go anywhere where they sent me. And I would go without question. All that, I said. And I meant it. But then I discovered really, even though I didn't say it aloud, that what I was saying to the Lord under my breath was this: "Anywhere, anywhere, but not Manchester or Leeds!" You don't know Manchester and Leeds. If you did, you would understand the parenthesis.[6] Ever caught yourself out doing that? You think you are completely surrendered. Our parentheses are often more felt than they are uttered. The little bits we slip in. They slip under our breath. But there are reservations on that total surrender. The moment you have that kind of parenthesis in your prayers you have fallen back from full surrender. And God must hold you to the parenthesis because that bit is not completely given up. That's why I had to have a ministry in Leeds[7] and spend a long time in Manchester as well. You can see why it must be. It must be!

My friends, take to heart the words of that lovely little Alsatian saint Etienne Mattier, who resolved the great dilemma of his life and said, "No questions Father, no questions, only amen!"[8] St. Francis de Sales used to teach his people to say to God, "Yes Father, yes and always yes!"[9] I had a little saint in my church when I ministered in Scarborough,[10] God bless her, who resolved all the problems of her own life with the same phrase. She would say at the end, when she'd had a little contention with God, she'd say, "All right, have it your own way Father." That's the way to live—*unconditional surrender*. "Have it your own way Father"—and no parentheses in our prayers.

---

6. Both of these large northern English cities had been centres of the Industrial Revolution, and were characterised by mills, factories, poor housing and slums. At the time of this sermon both cities were having to deal with a decline in manufacturing and lack of investment in industry and the reconstruction following the bombing raids of WWII. Since the mid 1990s both cities have developed thriving economies and have become attractive cities to live and work.

7. Sangster ministered in Leeds between September 1936 and July 1939.

8. Also Sangster, *Pure in Heart*, 151.

9. Sangster, *Pure in Heart*, 151. Sangster's reading of Francis de Sales seems to be reliant on Burton, *Life of St. Francis de Sales*. De Sales (1567–1622) became the Roman Catholic bishop of Geneve in 1602 and and became noted for his deep faith and his gentle approach to the religious divisions in his land resulting from the Protestant Reformation. He was renowned for his spiritual devotion and became famous for his spiritual writings, which focused on the importance of active love over penance as a means of spiritual progress. His most famous work was *Introduction to the Devout Life*, a devotional classic.

10. Sangster ministered in Scarborough from September 1932 until August 1936

Year ago there came to my house a young woman who said she had an important matter to discuss with me. She said, "Could she come in?" I said, "Come in." She came in and she said, "I work in the gas office in this town." She said, "The gas office in this town is the seat of iniquity. Oh, the stories they tell there. It would shock people in a factory. The gas office of this town is a terrible place. I work there and I know. I'm the only Christian in it." "Oh," she said, "I didn't come to tell you that. I came to tell that I'm called to the mission field and I want you to tell me how to go. I'm ready to go anywhere: to the heart of China"—China was open then[11]—"to the tip of Patagonia; to the coral islands of the south seas." She was ready, Bishop, had she been called to go to Fiji. And I said to her when she was finished, "You are totally surrendered to God, of course?" She said, "Why, of course! Didn't you hear me, the heart of China, the tip of Patagonia, the coral islands of the south seas?" "Yes," I said, "I remember that bit, but listen. From what you tell me about the gas office you appear to be God's only opportunity in that place. If God wants you to stay in the gas office, you're ready to stay, aren't you?" And she got up, and I could see the indignation in her face. She got up and said, "No I won't. I'll go anywhere, but I won't stop in the gas office."

How we Christians fool ourselves. Don't we fool ourselves? A moment before she'd been describing herself as totally surrendered, utterly given, "Ready for all thy perfect will,"[12] and a moment after, this great parenthesis, holding back, this denial of full surrender, this condition with God. "You take me out of this place and I'll be your servant." So, I say to you, my dear friends, "No conditions, please. Make no conditions of this character; none that limit your devotion. Make no conditions with God."

In the Methodist Church in Britain and in and other parts of the world, we have a lovely service, which finds no place, alas, in your rituals, and I'm saying this because I know we have a distinguished bishop in the congregation this evening [who]—and while I'm looking at you—I'm rather hoping he'll take this to heart. Now, in the Methodist Church in Great Britain, for two hundred years—we didn't invent it last week—for two hundred years we have been observing, on the first Sunday of every new year, a covenant service.[13] It was one of John Wesley's customs, in which we all listen, both in

11. Sangster is probably referring to the situation after the 1949 revolution in China, which saw a gradual tightening of controls on religion and the exodus of foreign missionaries.

12. This is the first line of the last stanza of Charles Wesley's hymn, "O Thou Who Camest from Above," from Hildebrandt and Beckerlegge, eds., *Collection of Hymns*, 473–74.

13. John Wesley first devised the covenantal service in 1755, an adaption of a Puritan devotion by Joseph and Richard Alleine. The 1781 edition of Wesley's service from his

our churches—oh, that blessed first Sabbath of the year—and the Methodist people in Britain rally and give themselves again to God. That wonderful two-hundred-year-old Covenant Service. It would be a wonderful thing if that could get known in our American Methodism too. And the culmination of the Covenant Service is a wonderful vow and it runs like this, listen:

> Put me to what Thou wilt.
>
> Rank me with whom Thou wilt.
>
> Put me to doing.
>
> Put me to suffering.
>
> Let me be employed for Thee,
>
> or laid aside for Thee.
>
> Exalted for Thee,
>
> or brought low for Thee
>
> Let me be full.
>
> Let me be empty.
>
> Let me have all things.
>
> Let me have nothing.
>
> I freely and heartily yield all things
>
> to Thy pleasure and disposal.

Wonderful words! Framed so completely that words could bear no greater set of meaning. My friends, you may not know the Covenant Service but you are in covenant relationships with God. Is that so? With that so, make no conditions, I beg you. Live in a state of unconditional surrender to heaven.

Here is the second assertion I want to make. Having said that, and eager as I am to be honest with you and not to send you away with any false notions, I want to remind you, painful though it may be to some of you, that God always, in his dealings with us, retains the right to say "No." We pray and normally we have the answers to our prayers. Isn't it so? Praying Hyde, when he worked out the percentage of yeses to his prayers, found, if I remember aright, that it came to 97 percent.[14] Mind you, that was Praying Hyde. He was

---

Short History of the People Called Methodists became the most utilised version. Though not well known or practiced in the US, hence Sangster's comments, this should not imply that the covenant service was entirely unknown in the US. It appeared in an edited and modified form in *The Book of Worship for Church and Home* in 1952. For a fuller discussion of the covenantal service, see Parkes, "Watchnight, Covenant Service and Love-Feast."

14. A missionary to India, John Nelson Hyde (1865–1912) became renowned as a man of prayer. During his missionary ministry in India from 1899 he began to commit entire nights in prayer, later forming the Punjab Prayer Union, the members of which prayed half an hour a day for spiritual revival. For further reading see Carré, ed., *Praying Hyde*.

praying in the Holy Spirit. He was praying for the right things. I want to say this to you: any of us with any length of days has known what it is to pray and beseech God, and in the end he said "No." You had that experience?

Did you have a boy who went away to the war and how you prayed for him, and did he not come home?

You had a dear one killed in a road accident?

Has somebody very precious to you been certified insane?

Then you know the awful, the vast distresses of life, the really big and terrible things. Have you? You surely have, hardly any of you with any length of days, that have [not] stood at some time beside the open grave. You know the experience of hearing God say "No."

My dear friends, this is what I want to say to you. We're making it to the matter we now have in mind. God retains the right to say "No." But, listen, listen, he's answering our prayers when he says "No." And listen, here's the wonder of it: he's in the negatives! These wonderful affirmations! And here's a wonderful thing—and I do want you to take this away with you this evening: it's possible for any one of you, who've taken God in your heart because of some big distress, some "No" he said to a fervent prayer—it's possible for you, here this evening, to leave that burden here in the auditorium. I'd love you to, I'd love you to. You can do this as you sit in your seat.

Listen! It's possible to change the character of a bitter cup, if you'll only change the hand from which you take it. And to change the hand from which you take it, you have only to change your mind. You think of our Lord in Gethsemane; Jesus had this experience of hearing his Father say "No." There he was in agony. He sweat blood. He said, "Father, if it be possible let this cup pass from me" [Matt 26:39]. It didn't pass from him. His Father said "No" to that pleading prayer. What did Jesus do? Oh listen, listen, this is what, as St. John tells us, what Jesus did: the moment he knew his Father willed it, he said, "I'll drink it." And then he said this: "The cup which my Father hath given me, shall I not drink it?" [John 18:11].[15] "Which my Father hath given me"!

Oh, but you say, "That's wrong! That cup was concocted by wicked men. It was Judas. It was Pilate. It was Caiaphas. They were the people who made that cup." Yes, they were and Jesus knew that better than you do. But it is as though he said that, "I won't take it from them. I won't take it from them! If I'm going to drink that cup I'm only going to take it from my Father, only from my Father." And only when he knew his Father wanted it, he said, "The cup which my Father hath given, shall I not drink it?" And he drank it.

---

15. There is no mention of the name Gethsemane in John's account, though the above words of Jesus bear parallels to the Synoptic tradition's prayer of agony in Gethsemane (Matt 26:38; Mark 14:36; Luke 22:42).

You see, if you are struggling against some darkness in your life, if there are the seeds of doubt in at least one layer of your mind, if you constantly recur in your thinking to: "Why is my one dear child retarded, my child?"; "Why has my father been twisted for eighteen years with arthritis?"; "Why have we never been blessed with children?" "Why?" Does that recur in some form or other? Some bitter cup! Could you not do this evening what your blessed Saviour did in Gethsemane? Could you not say, "I'm going to take it from my Father's hand"? He didn't do it, maybe, but he's permitted it. And listen, this is God's world at the last and God takes part responsibility not only for what he does but also for what he allows. He's allowed it! "The cup which my Father hath given me, shall I not drink it?" Oh come, I beg you, come. Why not do it now while you sit there? Come to unconditional surrender.

I may not know on this earth the meaning behind it, the ministry that could spring out of it. But I shall know in heaven. I'm going to trust him, and it will be entire trust. It will be utter devotion. You see how it's done? Hear again: you can change the character of a cup if you'll change the hand from which you take it, and to change the hand from which you take it you need only change your mind.

Oh, let me show it to you again in the Scriptures. You think of the Apostle Paul—what a mighty man he was. Oh yes! Oh, I had one son, and I called him Paul. What a man. And yet you know that God allowed Paul to be shut up in prison, and more than once, it seems. When he could have been swaying multitudes, when thousands could have been hanging on his word in a church here and there or somewhere, and God allowed him to be shut up in prison. I've often thought of Paul going into prison that first day. I can almost see him in my mind's eye. Paul at the prison gates and he looks up to heaven and says to his crucified Lord, "Jesus, are you going to allow this?" And then he catches one look from him, just one look, and it's all past. And when he caught that look, listen: Paul changed his imprisonment by changing his jailer. He changed his jailer! He did! How do I know that? Because he had a letter to write and he called to the amanuensis, the person that was to take it down, "Take it down, this letter," he says in prison: "Paul, a prisoner of Jesus Christ" [Phlm 1]. He was a prisoner of Nero, that inhuman monster, that wicked, wicked man and he never says it. In his thirteen letters to us and never once does he say he is a prisoner of Nero. No, no, he's changed his jailer. He changed it in his mind. You change the very character of your imprisonment when you change your jailer. "Paul, a prisoner of Jesus Christ." "Now it's up to you, Lord, to make something of this imprisonment. You're consenting to it. You'll turned it to good and it's your responsibility." He did. We all know that.

Some of the most precious parts of the New Testament would never have been written if Paul hadn't been locked up in prison. He was going to visit them but because he couldn't because he was in prison, so he sent them a letter and that letter has been the precious heritage of the church ever since.[16] Paul couldn't know that. We can look back how Jesus vindicated himself in the passing of the ages. Notice this: you can change your imprisonment if you will change your jailer, and to change your jailer you have only to come again to full commitment, to total surrender. Are you there? What's your imprisonment? Is it ill health; the kind of ill health that not even with faith you seem unable to step out of? Are you confined alone in difficult circumstances. Did you sign for the mission field and get held at home? What is your imprisonment? You can change your imprisonment if you change your jailer, and to change your jailer you only have to change your mind.

My friends, some time ago a dreadful accident happened on the mission field. We can talk of it now, though it was hushed up at the time. In a certain part of Africa the natives are not allowed to carry guns at all; you can see the wisdom of that. Europeans may, and missionaries may. And in this area of which I am now thinking, if any African village was being troubled by a lion they would go to the mission station and ask one of the missionaries, and one in particular, who was a deadeye with a gun, if he would come and shoot the lion. And their little group of elders came to the mission station and said, "Our village is troubled by a lion which is stealing our cattle and we fear for our babies. Would you please come and shoot the lion?" And the missionary said, "Why yes, I'll come." And he went, went through the bush, left the clearing and went towards the village, went all prepared as one seems one must be, it seems in the bush, with a bullet up the spout, as you men who served in the army will understand. What he didn't know was this: as he left the mission clearing his colleague's little son followed him into the bush, and went on following him. And as the missionary approached the village he heard a sound at the side and swung round and fired. And he shot his colleague's, his colleague's little son—shot him dead.

They told me afterwards of the scene in the bungalow of that bereaved father. The broken-hearted missionary, when he got back, flung his rifle down, went into his colleague's bungalow, fell down on his knees before his colleague and said, "O my dear colleague, my dear colleague, how will you ever forgive me?" And his colleague, utterly staggered with the awful news, put his hands on the shoulders of the man who had done the deed and said, "My dear brother, I am not dealing with secondary causes. I am dealing with God."

16. These are commonly understood to be the letters to the Ephesians, Philippians, Colossians and Philemon.

I am dealing with God—that's the heart of it. In the big troubles that have come to me in my life, such as they be, I want to be dealing with God not just with secondary causes. If I could get to God, if I can find God in it, I can get through. Look to God. Don't linger long on secondary causes. "Father, you didn't do it. You couldn't do it, but you've allowed it, Father. You've allowed it. And you wouldn't allow anything out of which at the last you can't work good." Deal with God. Deal with God.

Here is my final point and let me make it my briefest point. First, no conditions with heaven; it's unconditional surrender. Solemnly face the facts that God sometimes says, "No," but remember, there's always a ministry in it if he allows it. You will meet him in the heart of that sorrow and you can change its character if you will change the hands from which you take it.

And this finally and this chiefly: be unshaken in discipleship, my dear friends, whatever happens. I can tell you are Christian people, but in my ministry I've found that there are people who are Christian when everything is going well with them, when they were healthy and prosperous, when income balanced expenditure, and the children were well and growing up nicely—then they were Christian. And when things went wrong they weren't Christian. Oh, you're not there, are you? You are not people who would come aside to study the Word of God as we're going to do; you're not that kind of Christian. Be unskakeable in discipleship whatever happens.

I've told in one of my books how I came home one year from the Methodist conference rather jaded.[17] And you can return from a Methodist conference jaded. Some of you will be thinking that coming events cast their shadows before them. I came home from conference jaded and as I came into the house my dear wife met me and said, "Mrs. Johnson's been to see you." That's her name. This happened. "She's in trouble, dear. She wouldn't tell me what it is but she's in great trouble and she'll be here any moment." And then the bell rang. It was Mrs. Johnson who came through the door and she almost tumbled over the step. I said, "Come in Mrs. Johnson, you're in trouble." And when we were sitting together and the door was shut she said to me, "It's Jessie, it's Jessie." She had a daughter Jessie, aged then, I imagine about eighteen or nineteen, a lovely girl. I said, "Yes, Mrs. Johnson, I know Jessie. What about Jessie?" And she was almost incoherent in her grief. She said, "She's had some trouble with her eyes. I took her to the oculist. He told me this morning my girl's going blind. He said in three weeks she'll be blind. It would be better for me to tell her than for him. I can't tell my girl that. How can I? You tell her."

---

17. This story is related in Sangster's sermon "When Worn with Sickness," in *He Is Able*, 32–33, and the events to which Sangster refers probably took place in July 1930.

Those are the hard jobs that come to a minister of God. Would you like to be a minister in an hour like that? Oh, as tired as I was and hungry—don't linger if you've a hard thing to do. Do it at once—I got on the tram and dragged my way to St. Paul's Eye Hospital.[18] I can see now the little private room as I went in: the one bed, blinds drawn down, Jessie lying there. I didn't know what to say. I just talked about this and that, groping for an opening. And maybe I paused a little bit too long and she divined what I'd come to say and she broke the silence with this awful phrase; she said, "I believe God is going to take my sight away." What an awful phrase. And remembering what a missionary had said in hard circumstances years before, I said to her, "Jessie, I wouldn't let him." And she said, "You wouldn't let him? What do you mean?" And I said, "Jessie, do you think you could pray a prayer like this here? Not now, not in a week, but maybe in three weeks. Do you think you could pray a prayer like this?: 'Father, if any reason known to thee I must lose my sight, I will not have it taken from me; I will give it to you' Do you think you could, Jessie? Not now, dear. Not now. In three weeks, Jessie." I almost lived at that hospital for three weeks. I helped her with some difficult things, bless her. I remember the day when she said, "I can't say it! I can't say it!" I remember the day she said, "I can't. I can't live without a little light in this world." But as the last light faded, she said it and she meant it: "Father, if for any reason known to thee I must lose my sight, I will not have it taken from me; I will give it to you."

That's years ago now. I never go to Merseyside without seeing Jessie. She has a guide dog. You know, her eyes have a wet nose. He's a wonderful dog. Whenever they let him come into the church where I'm preaching he lies down in the aisle. And he gives me exactly twenty-five minutes for a sermon. I sometimes think he's got an alarm clock inside him. At the end of twenty-five minutes he stands up and loudly yawns. They can hear it all over the church. He'd have yawned tonight, wouldn't he, if he'd been here? You know how God has used that lovely girl's life? Oh, she's a woman now. She's one of the great speakers of Merseyside.[19] No one is more welcome at the women's meetings than is she. Out of the darkness she speaks of its light to those who hear her. Oh, what truth God tells her. He's told her things he's barely whispered to me.

18. The original building to which Sangster refers was a dismal brick building situated on Old Hall Street, Liverpool just a stone's throw from the old docks area. The hospital has continued as St. Paul's Eye Unit, Royal Liverpool Hospital and is situated near the city centre. Trams stopped running in Liverpool in 1957, though the journey from his home near Aintree would have taken around thirty minutes.

19. There was a considerable correspondence between Jesse, Jesse's mother and Sangster in the years that followed, the first letter being dated April 2, 1931. Jesse sent a letter nearly every year to Sangster thanking him for his part in coming to terms with her blindness. These are in the possession of the author.

Unshaken in discipleship. When something that seems like the worst happens, still unshaken, to you I say. I say it tenderly knowing the burdens that have fallen on some of you and death on others. My dear friends, be unshaken in discipleship, whatever happens. Unconditional surrender. Sometimes he says, "No," but there's a ministry even in the denial and I'm going on, I'm going on with him whatever happens, and what I do not understand on earth I shall understand above.

Let us pray:

> Almighty God, we have begun together, a company of friends.
>
> Set aside any premeditated word that is not thy word.
>
> Guide us all through this week.
>
> And thou hast blessed us so mightily in the messages
> of those who have spoken throughout this evening,
> most recently through Dr. Laubach and Dr. Graham.
>
> O God, speak with us still and,
>
> O may we be forever different because we have spent
> these hours with thee.
>
> For Jesu's sake.

Amen.

CHAPTER 2

The Doctrine of the Indwelling Christ[1]

THIS MORNING, IN THIS series of talks that I suggested to you last evening, I would take in these morning hours. I have never talked sequentially, in this way, on this theme before. It fills my mind, and I am proposing to write upon it because it seems to me to be a word to our age, but I want us to be so free with one another in these morning sessions. I want it to be, as it were, a cooperative effort between us. I am just going to open my heart to you on this, to me so central a theme. I may seem discursive to you at times. I will make no effort to be eloquent even if I could, or entertaining, which isn't in my mind. And if I know my own heart aright I haven't the slightest concern in what you think about me. But I have a very great concern that we all think aright about our Lord.

"We are Christian people," I said last evening. We have said "Yes" to God. Only Christian people would take their summer vacation in this way. We are Christian people, committed people, but is it total commitment? Is it, as we said last evening, *unconditional surrender*? How much are we in this way of life? We are Christians, but what kind of Christians are we?

My friends, we want to get deeper in. That's why we are here. I want to get deeper in myself. It is for those reasons that I intend in these morning sessions to direct your attention most specifically to what I would call "the Doctrine of the Divine Indwelling.

Now there isn't any doubt, I think, at all that many of us Christians are substandard Christians. We are living on a lower level than the New Testament teaches as normal. Oh, we are not now committing, if we ever did commit, the outward and grosser sins. We feel no disposition to run off with our neighbour's wife. We don't come home drunk. We don't use foul language. We're not fearing other people's good. And yet at the New

1. Parts of this sermon were later published in *The Secret of Radiant Life* ("Why Some Christians Are Not Radiant," 58–63; "A Man Who Received the Gift," 33–39; "How to Begin Clean," 185–87; "How to Get the 'We' in It," 200–201) and in *How to Live in Christ*.

28

Testament level we are substandard. We are fearful. We worry. John Wesley said, "I could no more worry than I could curse or swear."[2] But we worry. We are capable of jealousy. We discover ourselves in pride. We are inferior though we claim to be the sons and daughters of a king.[3] We are selfish and have our eyes constantly to the main "chance." We are Christians, but what kind of Christians are we? If Paul were to come into our company would he not think of us as he thought of that worshiping group of people he met one day at Ephesus?[4] He looked at them and he knew they weren't the real thing. He looked at them again and then he put his finger on it. He said, "Did ye receive the Holy Ghost when ye believed?" [Acts 19:2]. And they had not so much as heard that the Holy Ghost was given. They were strangers to what I call this "doctrine of the divine indwelling."

You will have often noticed with surprise at times that some people who are Christians, undoubtedly Christian in some ways, are rather miserable people. Sometimes you've been struck by it when you've been sitting in the official board and sometimes you've been struck by it when you're looking in the mirror. It's a curious thing that some of us that claim to be Christians and are in office do not sell the gospel by the life we live. There isn't any particular radiance about us. Supernatural love does not constantly stream out from us. The peace and serenity of God does not shine in us. Those are all marks of the indwelling of the Holy Spirit and we lack them. What kind of Christians are we?

Some years ago at an open-air meeting in the East End of London, which I know so well, an open-air meeting conducted by the Salvation Army, the officer was giving the address and one girl, recently converted, was scouting on the edge of the crowd. You know what I mean. She was going round the fringe of the people and if she saw anybody who was particularly interested she would just whisper something to them to discover whether they were seeking God. And a church official on his way home that Saturday evening paused at the meeting to listen to what the Salvationists were saying. He was a deacon from the Congregational Church, and felt a little superior to the Salvation Army. And he lingered there just to hear what they were saying. His face was all angry. You've seen those faces, as though there was a continually unpleasant odour under his nose. You know! You've seen faces like it. It had

2. This is an oft cited John Wesley quote that I cannot locate in Wesley's writings. In a letter to the author Randy Maddox says, "Indeed, JW almost never uses the word 'worry.' It may be someone's attempt to summarise something they found in Wesley, but I am certain that it does not appear in anything like this form in his sermons or other major writings."

3. Probably a reference to 2 Cor 6:18.

4. Acts 19:1–7.

set that way. And this little lass working round the fringe of the crowd went up to him and said to him, "Are you saved?" And you know, he was quite annoyed at being asked in the street if he was saved, and he—a church official—and he replied a little tartly, "Saved? I think I am." And the girl called over to the lass who was leading the meeting and said, "He says he hopes he's saved. What a face for a child of God!"

My dear friends, some of us might feel that that could be said with some relevance to even ourselves. Why doesn't it—if we're in this way of life, if God lives in us—doesn't that supernatural love stream out of us? Why doesn't that joy bubble in us? Why doesn't the peace and serenity of God shine through us?

We are Christians, but what kind of Christians are we? And I'm going to say right away that I don't think that the people who fail here—that church deacon, for instance—I do not think that they are hypocrites. Oh no. *Hypocrite* is a nasty word and ought always to be used with reserve. I do not think that they are hypocrites, by which I mean pretending to believe something that they don't believe. I think they are sincere and honest people. I think it of you, and with regard to that I could think it of myself. But those people who are substandard Christians are normally outside the great open secret of our faith. They're not, they're not enjoying this glorious mystery, this plain and practical and demonstrable thing: "the life of God in the soul of man."[5] They have the companionship of Christ, maybe. They do not have his indwelling. They are striving to be good by self-effort. They're living on their nerves and getting on other people's.

Surely there's a life of freedom from all that? A life in which, so we have read in the Testament—and that our fathers and mothers have testified to us—there is a life to be experienced in which God indwells the soul of his consenting servant. And you can think and feel and will with God, and walk with him, and do it not in your strained strength but in his strength. And wake each morning in the wonder of belonging to him and feel another day with God. Now, I call this deep truth the "doctrine of the divine indwelling." And, if you say to me why I think that it is so centrally important I will reply to you, "Just,

5. Sangster here seems to be alluding to Henry Scougal's (1650–77) classic book *The Life of God in the Soul of Man* (1677). Originally meant as a letter to a friend to explain the appeal of the Christian faith, permission was given to publish it as a book which quickly became a widely read classic Puritan devotional text. Scougal, a Church of Scotland minister and academic, depicted the Christian faith as a "Union of the Soul with God, a real participation of the Divine Nature, the very Image of God drawn upon the Soul." Jackson, "Scougal, Henry (1650–78)," *ODNB*. The text impressed the leaders of the eighteenth-century transatlantic revival. John Wesley reprinted the book in 1744, and later George Whitefield attributed his own conversion to having read a copy of the book lent to him by Charles Wesley years earlier. See Whitefield, *Works of George Whitefield: Journals*, 46–47.

because it is—because the Testament is full of it." If you doubt it, or by any chance have overlooked it, let me remind you of one simply thing.

The Apostle Paul, as you know, wrote under the Holy Spirit half the books of the New Testament. Thirteen of his letters have survived to us, just thirteen. They vary a good deal in size; one of them is little more than half a page. And yet they're so precious to us. We know the mind of the Apostle and we know the mind of our Lord through those thirteen precious letters. Now St. Paul, as you know, was a man of great intellect. He had been trained in the schools of the Gentiles and in the finest schools of Judaism as well. He ranked in the fore of all intelligent people as a great intellectual, and he had many things to say in his letters. And yet here's the strange thing: he says one thing over and over and over again. Wherever he begins he gets back to it. It's obsessional with him. There was one thing he said 164 times. Oh yes, in those thirteen letters, brief as so many of them are, there is one thing that Paul says 164 times. Oh, don't look surprised, my brother. I've counted it and I've checked Dr. Adolf Deissmann on the point and he makes it 164 as well.[6] Now, you count it, and if you make it 163, it won't matter. We won't argue over one. But Paul says 164 times one thing and it's this thing: "In Christ; Christ in me." "In Christ; Christ in me." I'll say it again. You comb his letters and see if it isn't true. Whatever he was talking about, this man who had so many things to say said one thing over and over again: "Christ in you" and "you in Christ." "If any man is in Christ he is a new creature" [2 Cor 5:17]. "I have been crucified with Christ, nevertheless, I live, yet not I, but Christ liveth in me" [Gal 2:20]. This was the thing that Christianity gave him and that Judaism hadn't given him. He had had a high moral code as a Jew and he struggled to fulfil it. And now, and now with a still higher moral code, he doesn't have to struggle in that same way. There is a power that has come into him and possessed him, and this was the thing that made him the apostle that he was—habited. In recurrent generations we Christians overlook this doctrine that was so obsessional to St. Paul and overlook the echo of it in all the wise writings of the generations since. Think of William Law,[7] one-time friend and

---

6. Sangster is reliant on the analysis of Deissmann, *Die Neutestamentliche Formel 'In Christo Jesu'* (1892). William Barclay provides an excellent summary and analysis of Deissmann's interpretation of Paul's "in Christ/Christ in you" and the subsequent biblical scholarship in response to Deissmann's views. Barclay, *Christ in You*, 5–19.

7. William Law (1686–1761), Church of England minister and devotional writer whose mystical and theological writings were influential in the developing evangelical movement of the eighteenth century. Law's *A Serious Call to a Devout and Holy Life* had a profound impact on the young John Wesley. From mid-1732 John Wesley corresponded with Law about reading, devotion and spiritual discipline. As John and Charles Wesley were exposing themselves to the Reformation principle of justification, particularly through the Moravians, around 1737–38 they began to feel Law's austere spiritual directives were heavy and joyless. John Wesley's letter of May 14, 1738 to Law accused him of

tutor to John Wesley. William Law said, "A Christ not in us is a Christ not ours." "A Christ not in us is a Christ not ours."[8]

The other day there died in England an old man, a friend of mine. He was nearly a hundred years old. He was a devoted Methodist and he had wonderful health. He was climbing our highest mountain when he had turned ninety. That was nothing to him. One time he suffered from rheumatism but he'd found a cure for rheumatism. Don't ask me for it afterwards because I don't know it. But he found what he thought was a cure for rheumatism. And certainly the people in Huddersfield where he lived and would see him struggling around for two or three years with rheumatism now saw him walking about with complete freedom. And they asked him for the cure and he gave it, gave it away freely. The only bother was this: that some of the people he gave it to still had their rheumatism afterwards. And he couldn't understand that. So, he enquired and discovered this: that although they'd asked him for the prescription they hadn't taken it. There are lots of people like that. They'll bother you for the prescription. Maybe you have a special prescription, you went to a specialist for it, you paid him $50. Your friend wants to know what it is—without the $50 of course. People are awfully interested in the prescription—but they don't always take it. Well, my old friend went on giving this prescription away. I've been there in his office and seen him type it out many a time. But after he made that discovery he always typed in capital letters on the top of the prescription, "THIS WILL DO YOU NO GOOD UNLESS YOU TAKE IT."

And I say, my dear friends, this glorious gospel of ours will do you no good unless you take it. You take it. Take it right in to you. Open your whole nature to the incoming of God. God has promised it.

> Come nearer Lord than near me,
>
> My succour to begin:
>
> Usurp the heart that claims Thee!
>
> O come and dwell within.[9]

Now it is just at this point that some of our fine Christian people, maybe somebody here this morning is missing their way. They have said "Yes" to God

---

setting an impossible standard that was ignorant of justification by faith. Also see Baker, *John Wesley and the Church of England*, 28. Sangster perceived William Law to be an Anglican Saint. W. E. Sangster, *Pure in Heart*, 76, 195.

8. The reference is "A Christ not in us, is the same Thing as a Christ not ours." Law, *Spirit of Prayer*, pt. 1, ch. 1, para. 43.

9. These are the last four lines of the final stanza of the hymn authored by Sangster in 1954 entitled, "A Prayer for the Divine Indwelling." See P. Sangster, *Doctor Sangster*, 258–59.

in their will and they meant it. They're not hypocrites. But they haven't opened their lives to God. There are people, earnest evangelists, who you may meet, who go about saying, "All you've got to do is believe. Only believe!" And if by their "only believing" they mean what I'm saying now, they're right. But so many of them when they say "Only believe" seem to think that it is the repeating of a formula or the uttering of a shibboleth. And that isn't enough. It's got to be a belief that opens your whole nature to the inflow of God. No man is changed, no woman, till they're changed in their mind. You listen to Paul again. He said, "Have this mind in you, which was in Christ Jesus" [Phil 2:5]. Listen again: "Be ye transformed by the renewing of your mind" [Rom 12:2]. It isn't enough to say, "Yes, I'll have him." He's to come into the mind.

You can see, my dear friends, all the more I think how important it is because the things from which we got deliverance—our grievous sins of the flesh, and sexual vices, if you ever had them, the tendency to this crudity or that—yes, where these things survive in us is in our minds, in the dirty little corners of our mind. There, we are self-centred; there, we are proud; there, we are envious; there, we are negative. There, in the corners of our mind we hold resentments of other people, utter insensitive innuendos, pass on that bit of scandal. I'm good, but I can do that. But you can't—if you do not have Christ in your mind. It is like a ship which has changed its flag but it hasn't altered the rudder. It's still on the old course although it's got another flag up. It's like one of those old castles in England which have changed hands in the war. There's another flag flying on the keep but the same dirty things are going on in the dungeons. Oh no, he's got to come right in, in every area of life to scour them out. His "refining fire," as the hymn says, must go through our hearts, our minds, "and sanctify the whole."[10]

So, how can we have the mind of Christ in us? You know, it isn't easy to put this quite plain. People are very practical people; like some of you, have proposed to lay it all aside for being mystical and unreal. Part of my task in these morning sessions is to put it so plainly and real to you that the hardest one among can say, "I see, I see your point."

Years ago after I preached a sermon on this theme, when my son was a little boy, he walked with me on the seashore on the Northumberland coast. And he said to me, "It is very hard to understand, Daddy. How we can be in

10. From Charles Wesley's hymn: "My God! I Know, I Feel Thee Mine," in *CHPCM*, 517–18. The full stanza is as follows:

"Refining fire, go through my heart,
Illuminate my soul;
Scatter Thy life through every part,
And sanctify the whole."

Christ and Christ can be in us?" I said, "It is son. It is." What would you have said to a little boy, nine or ten I suppose he was? What would you have said? How can you make mysticism like this real, for children? As we walked I saw a bottle on the beach. Some people had left it behind after a picnic. I picked up the bottle. I half-filled it with water from a pool. I stuffed the top full with dry leaves, so that it acted like a cork. And I went to the edge and I flung it out into the ocean. And it bobbed up and down and he stood there watching it. And I said to my boy, "You see son, the bottle's in the sea and the sea's in the bottle. And there it is bouncing along, bouncing along."[11]

My friends, it is a simple analogy. Maybe it will not serve your purpose; maybe we'll get deeper in than this: "You in Christ, and Christ in you." And then the mysticism of it becomes practical and we say, "How can the mind of Jesus be my mind?"

Listen, there are ministers of religion here, my own dear brothers, this morning, and they have been trained I suppose, most of them, in what we call counseling—what *you* call it here. We have other terms in England.[12] We all recognise that it's part of a minister's duty to give time to his people, especially when they're in perplexities. And if a minister doesn't do that he's failing in one of his serious duties. We know that lots of people wouldn't need a psychiatrist at all—if they came to their minister—further down the road. And he could sit with them and God could come into the conversation and the problem could be unraveled in that way. Now, you don't counsel people really in the deep things of the soul by just patting them on their back when they come with their troubles, and saying, "That's all right. Say your prayers. You'll be all right." That isn't the way of doing it. You must give them time. Oh, how many hours of every week during my long pastorate I gave to this work.[13] You meet them by appointment. They begin to talk—a problem on their life—you almost slip out of your own skin and slip into theirs. All your brain reposes in your ear. You're listening to the story. You only interrupt them just to make the point still clearer. "Give me this, give me this." And you

11. This illustration is related in the third person in W. E. Sangster, *Secret of Radiant Life*, 201. The story is taken from real events from the Sangsters 1938 summer holiday to Seahouses on the northeast coast of England, close to Lindesfarne. The author is in possession of a family holiday film from this vacation. The film documents them on the beach at Seahouses and two day trips; to Holy Island and to the Farne Islands. The Sangster twins would have been aged around eleven at this time.

12. In British Methodism pastoral counseling took place under the banner of "interviews" at this time.

13. Here Sangster refers to his time at Westminster Central Hall, which started at the outbreak of war in September 1939 and finished in July 1955. Paul Sangster provides only a short but nevertheless telling insight into his father's devotion to pastoral counseling in *Doctor Sangster*, 128–29.

talk with them. You try to get right into their mind. You pray. You say, "Let's be quiet. Let's now, both of us. We'll listen to God. We'll listen to God." You say maybe at the end, "I can't see the way, friend. I must pray about this. Oh you know, your confidence is safe with me. I must pray about this." And you have prayer sessions on your own. And you plead with God as you live in the life of that person in their need and you say, "Father, I've sifted it for pride, and I have sifted it for chronic selfishness, and I've sifted it for this or that, and all the peace and serenity but there's something bigger missing. Tell me what it is." And you meet them again and there may be a third time. And then! And then! By the power of God you come clearly. You put your finger on it. When you put your finger on it the assurance comes into their mind and they say, "Oh, I didn't know it was that. But I know it now. You were right."

Put that into reverse. Use that as a little second [source][14] to consider your commerce with God. You want to receive the mind of Christ. How can you hope to do it without the discipline of daily devotion? How can you hope to do it without intense staring at him, and staring at him there on the wood, with his bleeding side, and seeking to understand him in his Book and in personal experience, and, as it were, drawing in the very life of God by the traction of strong desire?

This is the way to it. I think, God helping us, we shall find a way this week how to open our nature to the inflow of God, how to feel within us the passionate power stronger than ourselves, how really to live the life of victory, how to find life is—even when it's beset with difficulties—still supremely good to have because that at the very centre of it we have him.

My friends here are the texts again: "Have this mind in you which was in Christ Jesus" [Phil 2:5]; "Be ye transformed by the renewing of your mind" [Rom 12:2]. How else? How else? If you are to be transformed it isn't enough to go on as you were. It isn't enough to change the flag and keep the ship on its course. He will come in, into every subterranean tunnels of the mind, into those wandering and sometimes lewd thoughts, into those ambitions that are so crude, right into the centre of our being, as we say within ourselves, "A Christ not in us is a Christ not ours."

Do you ever pose this question in your own mind?: "How is it possible for millions of people to live together in a big city and remain healthy, as they do in London, as they do in New York?" It is only possible by one of those overlooked miracles of modern life; that is, scientific sewage systems. They claim in London—with its enormous spread, with over twelve or thirteen

---

14. The recording is unclear here.

million people—they claim that our sewage system in London is one of the unnoticed marvels of the world.[15]

My friends, what happens to all the waste of a great city? We know it passes away in sewers and some of us are so nice but we don't like to talk about sewers. You better! You better! Sin belongs to the sewers, and it's with sin that we are dealing now. How is it possible for all the evil matter to pass out through the sewers and leave us to be uncontaminated, so that millions of people live together and they live a health life?

Well, I'll tell you this: some of the sewage is used as organic manure, and some of the sewage is used to produce a fuel gas. But always with sewage there is always an irreducible minimum at the last which is so evil that you can't do anything with it. You've got to get rid of it some way, somewhere, somehow. Now in London,—and they have them in New York—we have what we call "sludge vessels."[16] We have four of them in London. We call that evil matter, that utterly evil matter, we call it "sludge." And on every weekday tide on the River Thames, as on the River Hudson, two of these sludge ships—they're tankers—carrying 1500 tons and loaded with this poisonous and noxious matter. And they start down the river to the open sea. You can see them going. Just dirty little ships, some people might think them to be, but it's on their constancy and that our health depends. Down they go in England, down the Thames, right down past Southend, right out into the North Sea. And they go to a point fifteen miles beyond Foulness Island, where we have discovered a great big declivity in the surface of the ocean, and we call it "Black Deep."[17] Black Deep. And when the little sludge vessel gets over Black Deep all the bows are opened and within twenty minutes all that evil matter has gone away, down, down, down into the salt antiseptic sea, all its poison devitalised. Down

15. This was no idle claim or bias on behalf of Sangster, himself an avid Londoner. The capital's antiquated medieval sewage system had not been able to cope with the population growth and industrial developments of the early nineteenth century, with London becoming the largest city in the world. During the 1850s, therefore, efforts began to replace the overworked and inadequate system, which was the cause of much disease and a foul stench, with a modern network. The efforts and work of Joseph Bazalgette (1819–91), an imaginative engineer, led to the design of a modern sewer system, much of it still in use. Some of the pumping stations, no longer in use, are considered to be classic designs and architectural jewels, e.g., Crossness Pumping Station and Abbey Mills Pumping Station. See Cadbury, *Seven Wonders of the Industrial World*, 165–66, 189–92.

16. Known by their crew as "Bovril boats."

17. The first sludge boat was commissioned in 1887, named the Bazalgette after Sir Joseph Bazalgette, with all of them being withdrawn from service in 1998 following European Union directives on pollution in the North Sea. From 1967 until their withdrawal the sludge vessels used another deep part of the North Sea called Barrow Deep. See Salomons et al., eds., *Pollution of the North Sea*.

it goes, never to be seen again—never. And if you take a sample of the water from the surface of the water or from near the ocean bed half an hour later, it's pure. It's wholesome. It's uncontaminated. The work has been done. The great sea is healthy.[18] The sludge vessel carried it all away.

Listen, I know a deeper declivity for my sins and your sins than Black Deep. I do. Charles Wesley, he put it this way:

> O Love, Thou bottomless abyss,
> My sins are swallowed up in Thee
> Covered is my unrighteousness,
> Nor spot of guilt remains on me,
> While Jesu's blood through earth and skies
> "Mercy, free, boundless mercy!" cries.[19]

This is what I want us to do as we come to an end this morning. We've begun the quest for the "Indwelt Life." We are wanting [end of recording].[20]

This is the place for sin—the *only* place. Drop it in that bottomless abyss. There is nowhere else in the wide world where, being put, it will not remain active as evil. Only there can the sinful principle be broken, and only there has it really gone.

Some people go to God for forgiveness and profess to believe that they have it—yet seem never able to forgive themselves. They walk in shadows all their days because of something which God has pardoned and pledged himself to remember no more. But *they* remember it—and not only rarely (when a chance remark might unavoidably bring it to their mind), but regularly and with emotional turmoil, and of set purpose. They dwell on it, and seem to

---

18. Though the point of Sangster can still be taken this illustration is no longer viable in the light of contemporary environmental science, as the findings of the report *Pollution of the North Sea*, eds. Salomons et al., clearly demonstrates.

19. Third stanza from the hymn "Now I Have Found the Ground, Wherein" (in *CHPCM*, 308–9), from the German of Johann Andreas Rothe (1688–1758). Out of the original ten verses John Wesley translated vv. 1, 2, 4–6 and 10. Not an original hymn of Charles Wesley. See *CHPCM*, 308–9.

20. The recording ends at this point. In order to provide a link and continuity within the series, the final part of "How to Begin Clean" (in *The Secret of Radiant Life*, 186–87) has been selected as a substitute ending. The sermon seems most likely to have concluded with similar thoughts and admonitions, and also follows immediately after the sludge vessels illustration and the subsequent citation from Charles Wesley's hymn. Sangster also begins his next sermon, "How to Covet," by giving a brief summary of this sermon, concluding with, "We began yesterday on that quest and we began clean; washed in the blood of Christ. We loaded, as it were, the sludge ship with our sin: the gross and outward sins and the inward sins as well." So, it would appear that the sermon terminated with the thoughts related to the sludge vessels, as does the piece selected.

torture themselves with memory. They almost make the forgiveness of God of no effect. Certainly the pardon of the Almighty has failed to bring joy to their melancholy hearts.

It would shock them to suggest it, but they seem almost to imply that God's word is not to be trusted. If the protest that they *do* believe in God's forgiveness even if they cannot forgive themselves, they are unconsciously claiming to be more tender in conscience than the Holy God himself. If God takes a "light" view of sin, they can't! The unconscious blasphemy of it!

God has forgiven you. Let no one accuse you—not even yourself! Whenever that lying accusation rises in your soul, murmur aloud: "No spot of guilt remains on me." Who are you to make the blood Christ of no effect? How dare you suggest that God, who suffered crucifixion for sin, is too easy on a moral point? How comes it that when Christ would drop that deed of yours into the bottomless abyss you must snatch it from his pierced hand and keep it quivering in your unforgiving heart?

God has forgiven you! Forgive yourself!

Start again! Start clean!

Load the sludge vessel, in imagination, with your sin. Mentally place aboard all that God has forgiven—but which you find so hard to forgive yourself [. . .].[21] Put your worries aboard too. Toss on your pride. Bundle your resentments together; they can go as well. Make a heap of the unsavoury things [you find when you look][22] into the mirror of Christ. Picture yourself loading the ship with the lot. There it goes! It is on the way to Black Deep. It is going for ever and ever. And now recall that all your forgiven sins go into a deeper declivity than Black Deep.

Let us pray:

> O Love, thou bottomless abyss,
>
> My sins are swallowed up in thee
>
> Covered is my unrighteousness,
>
> Nor spot of guilt remains on me,
>
> While Jesu's blood through earth and skies
>
> "Mercy, free, boundless mercy!" cries.[23]

Amen.

21. The recording is garbled at this point.

22. As this admonition was not in the sermon but only in the book, the tense has been changed to create better meaning.

23. Taken from the conclusion of "How to Begin Clean," in *The Secret of Radiant Life*, 186–88.

CHAPTER 3

The Divine Call

HEAR THE WORD OF the Lord as it's written in the second letter of Paul to the Corinthians in chapter 11, beginning at verse 16. Hear the apostle when he spoke, as he himself said, "foolishly," but notice the record of his wonderful service.

[16] I say again, let no man think me a fool; if otherwise, yet as a fool receive me, that I may boast myself a little. [17] That which I speak, I speak it not after the Lord, but as it were foolishly, in this confidence of boasting. [18] Seeing that many glory after the flesh, I will glory also. [19] For ye suffer fools gladly, seeing ye yourselves are wise. [20] For ye suffer, if a man bring you into bondage, if a man devour you, if a man take of you, if a man exalt himself, if a man smite you on the face. [21] I speak as concerning reproach, as though we had been weak. Howbeit whereinsoever any is bold, (I speak foolishly,) I am bold also. [22] Are they Hebrews? so am I. Are they Israelites? so am I. Are they the seed of Abraham? so am I. [23] Are they ministers of Christ? (I speak as a fool) I am more; in labours more abundant, in stripes above measure, in prisons more frequent, in deaths oft. [24] Of the Jews five times received I forty stripes save one. [25] Thrice was I beaten with rods, once was I stoned, thrice I suffered shipwreck, a night and a day I have been in the deep; [26] In journeyings often, in perils of waters, in perils of robbers, in perils by mine own countrymen, in perils by the heathen, in perils in the city, in perils in the wilderness, in perils in the sea, in perils among false brethren; [27] In weariness and painfulness, in watchings often, in hunger and thirst, in fastings often, in cold and nakedness. [28] Beside those things that are without, that which cometh upon me daily, the care of all the churches. [29] Who is weak, and I am not weak? who is offended, and I burn not? [30] If I must needs glory, I will glory of the things which concern mine

infirmities. [31] The God and Father of our Lord Jesus Christ, who is blessed for evermore, knoweth that I lie not.

The first letter of Paul to Timothy in chapter 1 and verse 12:

> Appointing me to his service, though I was before a blasphemer and a persecutor and injurious. [1 Tim 1:12b–13]

Something precious goes out of the service of God when the sense of wonder in being in that service at all slips from our mind. Paul never lost that sense of wonder in being in God's service. It came to him first on the road to Damascus[1] or very soon afterwards. And it was with him still when he was composing his soul to die. He said to Timothy, his son in the gospel, "Appointing me to his service, though I was before a blasphemer and a persecutor and injurious" [1 Tim 1:12b–13].

Why did God call Paul? Why not some other young rabbi? There must have been some other rabbis as keen of mind, as strong in will, as devoted in heart. Why Paul and not someone else? Isn't there something mysterious in the call of God to his service? Is there anyone among us who can say, "God calls these people and not those people?" Is it possible for us this evening to understand the nature of the divine call?

I don't think it's possible for us fully to understand it. I'm going to say that as I begin even though I want to wrestle with that question this evening. There is something in it which I think will elude us even to the last. At the last, it is God's choice. He's on the throne. He chooses whom he will and he is answerable to none. I don't suppose that this is a rule among little American boys, but among little English boys when they play a game, it is always understood that the one who first suggested the game—or, as we say, "made up the game"—it is always understood that the one who first made it up is the one who should decide what other boys engage in it. And, if as lads, when we were in the midst of a game and another boy came along and said, "Can I play?," we always pointed to the boy who had made it up and we would say, "Ask him. It's his likes."

I lift that little memory of childhood to heaven and I say in the most reverent and sublime way that I can, "That God made this universe. That God created us, and at the last, 'It's his likes.'" He calls whom he will, I say. And, he is answerable to none. Nevertheless there is nothing of caprice about God, nothing of whimsy. I'm going to suggest to you this evening that while at the last there maybe something inexplicable in this, it is possible, if all of us together put our minds on this question, to settle quite definitely certain

---

1. Acts 9:22, 26.

things about the call of God. If we look at the men and women who he has summoned into his service through the generations, we can say, "Well, that doesn't matter, and that and that and that." But we can also say, "They all had these things in common. We can see the things that don't hinder the divine call, and we can see the things that are requisite for the divine call." And some among us, I trust, some young people especially, may go away, at the last, knowing that they also are summoned into his service and that these are the conditions they must fulfil.

Let us look then at the negative things to decide the things that don't matter. I'm going to say this quite definitely: past sin does not exclude us from the call to service. Let that sin be confessed. Let it be repented. Let it be forgiven. And past sin does not exclude you from the call to service. Isn't that wonderful? Some of the most magnificent servants of God had been, at some period in their life, great sinners. And they had come and confessed the sin and been forgiven and then, God called them to service. Past sin does not exclude you from this call to service.

All of us have sin in our life. Think on your sin. Was it flagrant sin or was it what some people call "refined" sin, though there's no such thing. Was it sin only known to Omniscience or was it sin known to the neighbours? What kind of sin was your sin? I don't mind what kind of sin it was this evening. I'm only saying this—with Paul in mind, the blood-stained Paul in mind—I'm only saying this: that whatever the sin was, if it was confessed and repented and forgiven, it is no barrier to the service of God. He loves to forgive. Oh how often I have opened the Holy Book and pointed it out to sinners and said to them, when they were coming to the cross, "God enjoys forgiving. He loves to do it! Look at it, it says so, 'He delighteth in mercy'. 'He delighteth in mercy'" [Mic 7:18]. Past sin does not exclude us from his service.

Some time ago I sat on a committee which had to appoint a man to an important post. We had just the short list to deal with. Each of the men came in in turn and we interviewed him. And when the last one had gone out we were all sure, I'm sure, who the man should be. There was one man that stood head and shoulders above all the others. I was sure whom I was going to vote for. And then before we could proceed to the vote one member of the committee rose and said, "Look, before there's any discussion on this I've something to say. I think you're all of a mind to appoint so and so. Now I'm going to oppose that and I'm going to tell you something." And then he told us an unsavoury story of this man's past. Oh, it had happened years ago. God, I am sure had forgiven him. I am sure of it. I'm sure, but this man hadn't forgotten and wasn't willing to forgive. He told us the story—most of us had heard it for the first time—and left us all inwardly distressed and wondering what to do. Men deal with us like that—men, though God himself says, "Your sins, will I remember no more" [Isa 43:25 and Heb 8:12]. Men, themselves sinners, remember our sin, have it ever before them. But not God.

My dear friends, I want to say to any among you who feels, "I would like to step out into God's service. I am now a forgiven man, a forgiven woman. But how can I with that behind me?" I say to you—remembering Peter,[2] and remembering Paul,[3] and remembering Augustine[4]—I say to you: past sin does not exclude you from his service.

Here's the second negative thing I want to point out: a lack of formal education doesn't exclude from his service. Now, don't discover in this any depreciation of education. I wouldn't be so foolish, least of all here. We all believe in education. If there is any young person here who is disposed to feel that doesn't matter, I beg you to think again. Yet, I am saying this: that a lack of formal education does not exclude you from the service of God.

Sometimes, those of us who love the Bible very much discuss with one another who was the greatest of the Old Testament prophets. I've often shared in those discussions. And always when that matter is discussed by people who really know, somebody is bound to put forward the name of Amos. You might judge him to be a minor prophet but many Old Testament scholars regard him as the greatest of the prophets. Amos, never mind the reasons that lead them to think that. I'm only saying this: that the man they put forward as the very first of that noble succession of Hebrew prophets was a man who described himself as "a herdsman of the fields, a dresser of sycamore trees" [Amos 7:14], a man denied the most education, the best education his age and race afforded, and he stands in the very front rank of all the prophets.

Somebody asked me some time ago what I regarded as the greatest evangelical movement in the world in the nineteenth century. "Observe," he said, "the nineteenth century." And after a little reflection I said, "Well, in the nineteenth century, in my judgement, the greatest evangelical movement in the world was the Salvation Army." And you will remember that the Salvation Army was begun under God by a man who had practically no formal educa-tion. William Booth had no formal education, really of the standards that we expect today, not at all.[5] Where did he get his education? In a pawnbroker's

---

2. This alludes to Peter's denial of Christ (Matt 26:34–35, 69–75; Mark 15:29–31, 66–72; Luke 22:31–34, 54–62; John 18:15–17, 25–27).

3. The story of Paul's persecution of the church is told in most detail in the Acts of the Apostles, with the story gathering force in its retelling. The repetition of the story before Agrippa paints by far the starkest picture (Acts 8:3; 9:1–2; 22:4–5; 26:9–11).

4. Augustine of Hippo's early sinful life is detailed in *Confessions*, first written in Latin around 397–400.

5. For further information about the life of William Booth, see Railton, *Authoritative*

shop. He was at work years before we would expect a boy to be at work today, and that kind of work—in a pledge office, listening to the hard-luck stories of people—that's where he got his education. And this was the man God used for the greatest evangelical movement of the nineteenth century.

The other day, hurrying through Epping Forest[6] to an appointment I had, I passed a little stone and I remembered who the stone commemorated. It was the stone put up as a memorial to Gypsy Smith,[7] near the spot where he was converted. And when Gypsy Smith was converted at the age of sixteen he could neither read nor write. He did his best to make up afterwards, but if you can't read or write at sixteen you can't become, in the rightest sense of the word, an educated man. And God used these people despite their lack of formal education. Ah, yes, that's what you say: "in spite of a lack of formal education." No! No! You've got it wrong, in some senses because of it, because of it. It was because he'd served in a pawnbroker's shop, when some people would have been at the university, that William Booth understood the poor. It was because he'd suffered deprivation that Gypsy Smith understood the poor. My friends, it isn't in spite of the lack of education, sometimes in the mysterious providence of God he turns our losses into dividends and makes even our disabilities yield an advance. So, I say to you, as important as education is, a lack of formal education doesn't shut you out.

I'm going to say this in the third place with regards to these negative things. There is no sex disqualification in the service of God. We sometimes claim for America and England that we now have full sex equality. But I wonder if that's true. The militant feminists, in my country, don't think they have

---

Life of William Booth (2007), and Hattersley, *Blood & Fire* (1999). Booth authored a number of books, the most famous of which was *In Darkest England and the Way Out* (1890). Contemporary scholarship of the roots of the Salvation Army highlight the significant role of Catherine Booth, deeming her cofounder of the movement. See Reed, *Catherine Booth*.

6. Epping Forest is an ancient forest to the northeast of London.

7. Rodney Smith (1860–1947) was a well-known British international singer and evangelist. Born into a traveller family in Epping Forest, hence his name nickname "Gypsy," Smith was converted at the age of sixteen in a Primitive Methodist chapel. After a short spell with the Salvation Army, Smith began an association with the British Methodist Church, through which he began his international ministry, later becoming good friends with Dwight L. Moody and Ira D. Sankey. He toured America numerous times, plus Australia and South Africa. He was in America when his wife died in England in spring 1937. Just over a year later, he courted some scandal by marrying his secretary, who was fifty years younger. Smith died on the *Queen Mary* on August 4, 1947 on his way to New York. "Gypsy Smith was probably the best-known and most successful international evangelist of his day. His colourful personality and fine tenor voice made him a strong pulpit attraction." Vickers, "Smith, Rodney [called Gypsy Smith] (1860–1947), Evangelist," *ODNB*. Also see Lazell, *Gypsy from the Forest*.

full sex equality. They're campaigning now for the same pay for the same work.[8] And I was talking recently with a woman doctor of medicine, a clever woman—took a couple of gold medals when she was going through the schools. Brilliant, without a doubt, and she's been practicing in a certain town for a number of years and she said to me, "Oh yes, I did well at the university but a woman doctor isn't everybody's cup of tea." That's how she said it. If she was here she would have said, "not everybody's cup of coffee," but we'll let that go. She said, "A woman doctor is not everybody's cup of tea." She said, "Men don't like a woman doctor." She said, "They only consult me really for the children's ailments and certain women's diseases." "Oh no, no!," she said, "never mind my university record." There isn't really sex equality in medicine.[9]

Some of you will know the name of Dr. Maltby,[10] one of the most distinguished Methodist ministers in Britain of recent years, and I remember him saying whimsically once, "Whenever God wants something done, he doesn't appoint a committee; he sends a man, and sometimes the man is a woman." Of course, of course, when God wants to make a saint he doesn't

8. Sangster is probably referring to the campaign for equal pay that gathered force after WWII and was particularly in the news in 1955–56. In Britain a vigorous campaign was pursued by the Equal Pay Campaign Committee until 1955. First hopes were for equal pay for women teachers and civil servants, based on the express conclusions of the 1946 report of the Royal Commission on equal pay. A year prior to the preaching of this sermon, a statute was passed to create equal rates of pay for men and women doing equal work in the non-industrial civil service. Both in the case of women civil servants and teachers, the full outworking of the decisions only took place in 1961–62. It is hard to establish Sangster's view on this matter, though his application of the term "militant feminists" to the subject of equal pay could either reflect general feelings in the 1950s towards women's roles and status among the larger populace or an underlying sexist stance, though none of Sangster's writings speak derogatively of women or their rights. See Davis, "Historical Introduction to the Campaign for Equal Pay."

9. In reference to the previous footnote, this illustration could actually indicate that Sangster felt that there should be sexual equality.

10. Russell Maltby (1866–1951), a British Methodist minister belonging to the Wesleyan Methodists before the 1932 Union, and best known for being the leading figure in the Fellowship of the Kingdom, a movement which drew ideas from Romanticism and liberal theology and combined these with central Christian ideas of the cross, the importance of Scripture, personal conversion and social and political activism. The group were highly influential in British Methodism between 1920 and 1950. For further reading on the Fellowship of the Kingdom, see Randall, *Evangelical Experiences*, ch. 5. Sangster's book *He Is Able* reflects a Christological approach similar to that of the Fellowship of the Kingdom, reflecting some involvement with the group.

only make a St. Francis,[11] he makes a St. Teresa.[12] When God wants to clean up the prisons he doesn't only use John Howard,[13] he uses that wonderful woman Elizabeth Fry.[14] When God wants to bring light into dark Africa he

11. Francis of Assisi (1181/82–1226), a Roman Catholic friar and preacher, devoted to a life of poverty and identification with the plight of the poor. He founded four religious orders, best known of which is the Order of Friars Minor (Franciscans). He was canonised by Pope Gregory IX in 1228. Numerous stories of miracles have been attributed to him, including him having a special relationship to animals. He is widely venerated across church traditions. See Cross and Livingstone, eds., *Oxford Dictionary of the Christian Church*, 635–36.

12. Teresa of Ávila (1515–82), Roman Catholic Spanish saint and mystic, belonging to the Carmelite order. Her mystical experiences and writings have proved highly influential, most notably *The Way of Perfection* (c. 1565) and *The Interior Castle* (1577), which developed a mystical theology of prayer as ascent of the soul, with ecstatic and sensual language flourishes. See Cross and Livingstone, eds., *Oxford Dictionary of the Christian Church*, 1600–1601.

Sangster's books *The Pure in Heart* (1954) and *The Secret of Radiant Life* (1957) and his pamphlets *You Can Be a Saint* (1957) and *How to Live in Christ* (1957) drew inspiration from Teresa's spiritual practices, with particular focus on the importance and experience of divine love as crucial to the pursuit of holiness; what Sangster termed "saintliness" in his later writings.

13. John Howard (c. 1726–90), British philanthropist and penal reformer, with a monument in honor of his life in St. Paul's Cathedral, London. Throughout his adult life Howard conducted research on the conditions of the poor and rights of prisoners in British prisons, petitioning Parliament for change. In his 1777 work *The State of the Prisons* his findings were based on visits to over three hundred places of confinement, detailing abuses and suggesting better forms of practice. See Morgan, "Howard, John (1726?–90)," *ODNB*.

14. Elizabeth Fry (1780–1845), British philanthropist and penal reformer and devote Quaker. Fry's conviction was that education could change society, most particularly the plight of the poor and prisoners. She is best known for her work with and for women and children in prison. Prompted by a family friend, Fry visited Newgate Prison (a former prison and London's largest, and place of execution, located on the corner of Newgate Street and the Old Bailey) in 1813, where the conditions appalled her. Returning, when able in 1816, she established meetings with the prison authorities. According to De Hann, "Fry and her female collaborators introduced a system of classification of the prisoners, prison dress, constant supervision by a matron and monitors (chosen from among the prisoners), religious and elementary education, and paid employment." Remarkable transformations in the conduct of prisoners was recorded. Fry set up a visitation system whereby she or one of her helpers visited Newgate on a daily basis. Following her own religious convictions, Fry read the Bible to prisoners each Friday. See De Haan, "Fry, Elizabeth (1780–1845)," *ODNB*.

doesn't only send David Livingstone,[15] he sends Mary Slesser.[16] Glory be to God! There may be sex disqualification still in many walks of life but there is no sex disqualification in the service of God. If there's any dear girl here this evening either side of me who feels, "I would love to give myself to the service of God. I wish I was a boy," oh my dear lass, you don't have to say that. You give yourself to the service of God as you are. You are as he made you, and as he made you, he can use you.

And here's my fourth negative. Isn't this wonderful? Physical disability doesn't exclude you from the service of God. My friends, sometimes physical disability does exclude you from human service. Just before Dr. Benson Perkins[17] and I came here to America we were sitting in our own Methodist Conference there in England and I'm sure that he went through the same pain I did. We have it every year. When the young men come before to be accepted for the ministry, we have their records all here. Here they are, 145 of them have offered this year and 109 of them have passed. But always there are a few in a special category. We look their figures over. "Oh yes, done brilliantly in Bible knowledge, in Christian theology, records of his sermons—splendid,

15. David Livingstone (1813–73), Scottish explorer and missionary. In 1840 Livingstone was assigned by the London Missionary Society to Kuruman (North Cape, South Africa) to a mission station founded by Robert Moffat in 1821. As a missionary he worked as a preacher, doctor, builder and printer but developed, ahead of his time, a more acute, and more tolerant, understanding of African customs and beliefs, believing that the LMS should train more native evangelists and teachers. Livingstone is often considered as Africa's greatest missionary, yet he is recorded as having converted only one African. Livingstone believed that his greatest spiritual calling was to open up the interior of Africa in order to find possible trade routes which would displace slave trade routes. His explorations attracted much interest in Britain and Livingstone became an honorary member of the Royal Geographical Society. His efforts led to the identification of numerous watercourses and lakes including Lake Ngami, Lake Malawi and Lake Bangweulu, but most notably Victoria Falls, where a statue is erected to his memory. His work inspired a missionary zeal for Africa in the late nineteenth and early twentieth centuries. His grave is placed in Westminster Abbey. See Roberts, "Livingstone, David (1813–73)," *ODNB*.

16. Mary Slessor (1848–1915), Scottish missionary inspired by the missionary zeal from the life of David Livingstone. In August 1876 she sailed for the Gulf of Guinea to work as a teacher in Akwa Akpa, Nigeria, after only three months' missionary training. She is known for rejecting colonial ideas, living off the land like the indigenous peoples and tackling the primitive superstition which led to tribal leaders killing twin babies. See Birkett, "Slessor, Mary Mitchell (1848–1915)," *ODNB*.

17. Ernest Benson Perkins (1881–1974), British Methodist minister who devoted the earlier part of his ministry to inner-city missions in Sheffield and Birmingham, the consequence of which led him to develop a special interest in opposing gambling and its social effects. Perkins became president of the Conference in 1948, vice president of the British Council of Churches in 1952–44, and moderator of the Free Church Federal Council in 1954. He coauthored *The Methodist Church Builds Again* (1946). See Greet, "Ernest Benson Perkins."

look: three Ones.[18] That's the highest distinction we can give men in England, "three Ones." A one for all his sermons. "This man's a preacher." And so we go through the record and we're already to say, "Yes, yes, we'll take him," when up gets the secretary and says, "Please, before you vote, I have a word to say. The doctors object to him on medical grounds." Oh dear, oh dear, for we all in the Methodist Church in England—and it is doubtless true to you here—we have to pass a most rigorous medical test. They require 100 percent fitness for us. They want forty years work out of us and it's hard work going round those circuits. And they can't take a risk on a man that isn't 100 percent fit. And here's a man with a line of marks like that and then the doctors say, "You can't take him." And we sit there so sad; "disqualified on medical grounds!"

Do you know, I've sometimes wondered if we would have taken the Apostle Paul into the Methodist ministry in England. I do, I do. He had a sickness. We don't know to this day what it was. It was a physical ailment. He called it a "stake in the flesh" [2 Cor 12:7–9]. It was recurrent; it came again and again. He never got delivered from it. Some scholars think it was malaria, some think it was ophthalmia, and some think it was epilepsy. We just don't know. But he had it and he had it to the end. He wouldn't have passed our tests to the Methodist ministry in England. Glory be to God, he passed God's tests. God took him in.

My dear friends, there's no physical disqualification in God's service. It might affect the form of service you do but it doesn't shut you out from his service. I mentioned St. Teresa just now, that wonderful saint of God. And it will interest every woman here to know that St. Teresa suffered all her life from terrible headaches. Do you know what she used to call them? "My rushing waterfalls in the head." Ever and anon in her writings you would find her work interrupted for a season and she would say, "Oh, these rushing waterfalls in the head."[19] But that didn't exclude her from God's service.

Did you ever hear the name of Dick Sheppard? A distinguished minister we had among us in England, died not long ago: a martyr to asthma.[20] Oh, how often I've seen him in the little waiting room before we go in to address

---

18. In the UK a "First" or "One" corresponds to a mark of A or A+.

19. Teresa of Ávila, *Interior Castle*, 67.

20. Hugh Richard Lawrie Sheppard (1880–1937), British Anglican minister who, following a time as hospital chaplain in France in WWI, first became known for his time as minister at St. Martin-in-the-Fields Church, off Trafalgar Square, London, followed by service as dean of Canterbury Cathedral. Throughout the 1920s and 30s Sheppard agitated for a recognition of the importance of every human life and the immorality of war. Sheppard was not blessed with good health, experiencing numerous breakdowns through a combination of overwork and asthma. See Wilkinson, "Sheppard, Hugh Richard Lawrie (1880–1937)," *ODNB*.

a great mass meeting, and his name could fill most any hall. And he couldn't get his breath, and he'd be struggling and say, "Wait a moment." And he'd pull out from his pocket a little instrument and pump oxygen or something into him, and then he'd say "Right." And off we'd go. That audience wouldn't know the struggle that good man was having. They wouldn't know it. He'd pour out his soul for God, stagger off the platform again, and need all our help to get him ready to go home. Oh, at what physical cost the servants of God have sometimes done his work.

And now listen again. Oh, apply this to yourselves as you may. Past sin does not exclude you from his service, so long as it be repented and forgiven. And a lack of formal education does not exclude you from his service, though get all the education you can. And listen, there is no sex disqualification in his service and physical disabilities do not shut you out. So brace yourselves in hope and expectation while I turn now to the positive side and point out what I judge to be the things you must have if you will receive the call of God.

My friends, I think I will put it to you in a series of questions. Maybe that will make it simpler for you. I'll just ask you the question and you just measure up to it in your own mind. Here's my first question on the positive side: Do you respond readily to God's touch? Do you respond readily to God's touch?

We vary in spiritual sensitivity. We vary in many things. We vary in the gift of music. There are some people sitting here on the platform who can find music in everything. Well, we'll judge that later when we've heard the "Hallelujah Chorus." Well, that's our hope concerning them; that they really are musical souls. And we know our musical director is, we know. There are some people just born with the gift and they find music everywhere. There are some people who find beauty everywhere. They don't even have to go to Lake Junaluska to find beauty. They can see it in a back yard. And it's there because they have the eye that sees it. But listen, while can't help to some extent that we're sensitive to music and sensitive to beauty, we can all of us help; as I explained this morning, we can all of us help how sensitive we are to the touch of God. You regulate your own sensitivity to him if you're deep in his Book, if you do not scamp your prayers, if you go when you have opportunity to the Holy Table, if you find yourself constantly in the Christian fellowship, if you use, in short, all the means of grace. You sensitise yourself to God's touch and when he touches you, you know it's God and you say, "I'm here, Father." And when he whispers in your ear you know it's God. You say, "I am listening Lord to thee. What hast thou to say to me?"[21]

So I ask you, do you respond readily to God's touch, or is this the fact: that God has called you and you have said, "Not now, Lord. Presently perhaps?" And then he's called you again and you've said, "Well, not that, Lord. Think up something else and I might." And then! And then! He goes and calls someone else. If you get to heaven it will be a shadow on the joys of heaven for you that you were deaf to his repeated call and indifferent to his claim to service. Do you respond readily to his touch? There's my first question. And remember, you can yourself regulate your sensitivity to his touch.

Here is my second question: [Will you take your wages from God alone?][22]

[. . .][23] But some people engage in Christian service ostensibly for the pure glory of God but, "I really want a good deal of human praise as well." Every minister here has had the experience, I'm sure, of people who come and resign from this job in the church or that. And they don't really want to resign. They only want to be told, "What a good job you're doing. Oh, you're just wonderful, wonderful. We couldn't get on without you. You just go on." And they take the resignation back and just go on. They're just screwing a little bit of praise out of it. I classify resignations now as "A" and "B" resignations. "A" when the fellow really means it, "B" when he doesn't and only wants to be told what a good chap he is.

My dear friends, I beg you, I know that a little bit of praise does us good at times. I know that. But you'd be surprised, in England, how niggardly[24] our people are with praise. Oh yes, mark you, if you, if you don't "break the bread of life"[25] quite cleanly to them sometimes, they'll tell you that. But you can go an awful long time before they'll tell you, you do. It's the reserve of our nature. It's the reserve of our nature.

But, my dear friends, welcome as though a bit of encouragement is sometimes, fancy people being willing to resign from the service of God because men do not praise them. Praise is like perfume; a little whiff of it now and then is good, but don't drink it, don't drink it.

---

hymn "Master Speak! Thy Servant Heareth."

22. The recording is damaged here. This question is reconstructed from his conclusion of this section.

23. The recording is damaged here and a short section, perhaps one sentence, is missing.

24. Meaning miserly or ungenerous.

25. Common designation in evangelicalism for the act of preaching, from John 6:35, where Jesus refers to himself as "the Bread of Life."

Did you ever here the name of Fred Banting,[26] the man that discovered insulin, which gives every poor diabetic a reasonable chance at life? Did you ever hear his name? Banting was a young man. The year was 1919, not long ago. He was a lecturer, only a part-time lecturer in the Western Ontario Medical School. And one night a great thought came to him, something that might help poor diabetics, people suffering from the awful sugar sickness. And at the end of term, just before the long vacation began, he went to Toronto and sought an interview with Professor McCloud, the professor of physiology. The professor was just going to Europe, and in a hurry, and wondered what this young man wanted. "What do you want, young man?" And Fred Banting began to stumble out he thought he'd got an idea for something that might help diabetics. And the more he spoke, the more astonished the professor looked. And when Banting paused the professor said, "Do you think, a young man like you, that you will make a discovery which has eluded the greatest physiologists of all ages?" That's a difficult question to answer. You see, if you say "Yes" it sounds proud. If you say "No" he'll say, "What are you wasting my time for?" So, poor Fred Banting didn't know what to say. And he said nothing. He just stood there in the presence of the great man. And, because the great man was in a hurry, he said, "Look here young man, what do you want?" And Banting said, "I want a trained assistant, Sir, and laboratory, during the long vacation, just to try out this idea. Would you mind?" And that professor will be forever famous because he gave Banting what he asked for—just that. It wasn't really a laboratory; it was a cubby hole under the stairs. I've been there. And it wasn't a trained assistant; it was a medical student, Charlie Best, though he proved to be a great man.[27] And off went the professor to Europe. And those two boys—they were little more than young boys—they went to work, and they did it! They did it! They made the discovery that eluded Langerhand and Opier and all the others that had worked on diabetes. They found insulin. They called it "isulatin" but that was bad Latin so it had to be improved. And we've called it "insulin" ever since. And when the news went round the world, oh, the astonishment everywhere. And the British Medical Association was in session at the time, and when they heard of it they passed a solemn resolution in London congratulating Professor McCloud and his assistants on the wonderful discoveries they'd made. The professor was still in Europe. And Charlie Best opened one of the papers in

26. Sir Frederick Grant Banting (1891–1941), Canadian physician, researcher and Nobel Prize winner (1923) attributed with the ideas and research that led to the isolation of insulin (1921). See Bliss, "Banting, Sir Frederick Grant (1891–1941)," *ODNB*.

27. Charles Herbert Best (1889–1978), decorated American physiologist and researcher who aided Banting in isolating a pancreatic extract of insulin. He went on to have a distinguished career in medical research. The Charles H. Best Foundation set up in his honor supports medical research.

Toronto the morning after and read this and said, "Fred, the British Medical Association are congratulating Professor McCloud. What do you know about this?" Now listen to what Fred Banting said, for this is my whole point in telling you the story. This is what he said, he said, "Charlie, it doesn't matter who gets the praise so long as the poor diabetics get the help."[28]

Wasn't that noble? Now that was the man. Mark you, we caught up on that mistake later. Banting got a knighthood: he was Sir Frederic Banting.[29] Banting got the Nobel Prize. The truth came out. Thank God! But the thing I always like to remember about him was that, that in the very hour that other people were getting the praise and his name wasn't even mentioned, he said, "It doesn't matter who gets the praise, so long as the diabetics get the help."

My dear friends, let me say this to your face: it doesn't matter who's second, so long is Jesus is first. You are advanced in grace when you can go on working for Jesus if nobody praises you. The Master praises mortal men. And look, you're still more advanced in grace when you can do a job and hear somebody else praised for it, and still be glad that it's been done for Jesus. You can do anything you like in this world—if you don't mind who gets the praise.

So, I'm asking you—this is my second question: Will you take your wages from God alone? Though people are chilled[30] towards you, if he smiles and says to you, "Well done, son," make that your whole reward. And though all the world is praising you, if he turns his face away, think nothing of the plaudits of the world. Live with a single eye to God. Make his praise your whole aim. Take your wages from God alone.

Here's my third question, and I'm done. The first: Do you respond readily to his touch? Will you take your wages from God alone? Will you go right on to the end? You know, there are times in life when it's difficult to go on. Some years ago I had recently read the papers. It was almost too painful to tell. One of our missionaries was sent home from the West Indies. You know we have great overseas missions in the West Indies. We've had them there for more than a century. Years ago we had a missionary who had befriended the slaves against the worst kind of the planters. And he became their friend, and they loved him for his friendship. And he became their spokesman and defender.

---

28. Sangster's version of the story conflicts somewhat with the account of Michael Bliss, Banting's biographer, who says, "Banting, who never understood the extent to which the emergence of insulin relied on a well-supported collaborative effort begun with his faulty idea, fought for and received acclaim as the primary discoverer." Bliss, "Banting, Sir Frederick Grant (1891–1941)," *ODNB*.

29. Banting received his knighthood in 1934, the last round of knighthoods given to Canadians. Bliss, "Banting, Sir Frederick Grant (1891–1941)."

30. This carried a different meaning to the modern usage. Sangster really means "ignore."

And then their opponents, the people that were grinding them down, worked a trick and got among those slaves and persuaded them that, so far from being their friend, this missionary was secretly their enemy. In the language of today, he was really "double-crossing" them. And they believed the lie and they themselves hounded that good man out of the islands. He came back to England a broken man, and listen to what he said: "It is one thing to suffer for the people; it is another and a worse thing to suffer by the people." I remember that whenever I hear the crowd shouting to my Lord on the cross, "Crucify him, crucify him!" [Luke 23:21]. The bitterness of it. On Sunday they said, "Hosanna!" [Matt 21:9] on Friday they say, "Crucify!" [Matt 27:23]. "It is one thing to suffer for the people; it is another thing to suffer by them."

Will you still go on loving and serving despite the suffering and the obloquy? And listen, will you go on loving and serving even to old age, when people have forgotten you; when a generation arises "that knows not Joseph" [Exod 1:8]? Will you still love and serve him though the eventide is difficult and penurious? Will you still be constant to the very end of the road?

When I was a lad the greatest missionary of our society was a man on the west coast of Africa. By the way, whoever drew up this map in the little chapel behind me, with Methodism's world mission on it, ought to draw it up again. Because you've left out so many of the most glorious mission stations our world Methodism has. You have. Let me help you. I looked. It isn't coloured red at all; no mark there where such magnificent missionary service is being done. I looked at that "white man's grave," Sierra Leone. I looked at the town of Freetown.

My dear friends, in Freetown there's a Methodist chapel. There it is, and there's a long path that goes up to it. And there's a line of graves on both sides and there's a young missionary in every grave. They all came from my old college.[31] We built our church in the white man's grave on the bodies of our dead missionaries. We knew nothing about tropical diseases then. Some of them died on the boat. Many of them didn't live a month. And the cable would come back to the college of a man that had only been rolled off a month or two before. The principal would come in with the cable in his hand for prayers. Everybody knew what it was. And after prayers he'd say, "Gentlemen, I'm so sorry to tell you that our brother so and so, whom we sent to Sierra Leone two months ago, has laid down his life for our Lord. And the church asks Richmond to send another man." And before he could get out of the chapel they were pulling his coat tails to be the next to go.

I say, we built our missions there on the bodies of our dead missionaries. But there was one man who outlived them all. He stayed there over thirty years,

31. Cumbers, *Richmond College 1843–1943*, 22.

an incredible man. He learned their language, reduced it to writing, translated the Testament, and every little while he would come home. When I was a boy how we gazed in wonder at that man, and he'd bring armfuls of gods that had been superseded and told us of the triumph of the gospel. And he only died the other day, practically forgotten. Oh, the mission house knew of him. They wouldn't forget. But our church in Britain—I say it with some pain—forgotten. "A generation," I say, "had arisen that knew not Joseph" [Exod 1:8]. And I wouldn't have known this story but for the chance meeting with a nurse. He died in a hospital in Buckinghamshire, an old man, who had lived a widower to a great age, and hurried into this hospital. And the nurses were talking one day in the nurses' common room, and one said to another, "Isn't that man in so and so ward a funny man? He has an English name but sometimes he doesn't talk English. And I think he says his prayers in a strange language sometimes. And when he's in delirium he says the funniest things." And this dear girl, herself a Methodist, and noticing the name, went and discovered this old man, this old, old man, this great man at the margin of the river. And she said, "Mr. So and So, I know who you are. I know who you are." And he said, "You do, my dear. How kind of you to come. I would like somebody to pray with me. Now look, let us say the Lord's Prayer together. You say it in English and I'll say it in the language I've loved so long on the west coast of Africa." And together they said the Lord's Prayer. Never a regret in his heart. No complaint that he was overlooked. His eyes fixed on Jesus, catching the smile of his Lord, saying with Charles Wesley, "O let me catch one smile from Thee, and drop into eternity."[32] And he caught the smile and dropped into eternity—gloriously indifferent to the praise or blame of men. What does that matter?

Do you respond readily to his touch? Will you take your wages from God alone? Will you go on in unshaken loyalty to the end? Will you? Then, give yourselves. You young people especially, give yourselves into his royal service. And with hallelujahs ringing in your ear say, say to God in your heart, "I'm ready Lord. You will appoint me to your service. I am ready to obey."

Let us pray:

O God, our Father,

we marvel at thy willingness to us human agents at all,

and yet that is thy way.

Use us, despite our sin, and despite our disabilities
of mind or body.

---

32. The final two lines from Charles Wesley's final poetic verse dictated on his death bed, "In Age Feebleness Extreme."

Use us, and make us such men and women as are truly dependable.

For thy name's sake.

Amen.

CHAPTER 4

How to Covet[1]

[WELCOME TO][2] THE SECOND of these talks on what I have called "the quest for the Indwelt Life." Yesterday we agreed that we are all unworthy. We were Christians. We had said "Yes" to God. But we fell to wondering what kind of Christians we were. We wanted to get further in. We agreed that the central doctrine of Paul's letters is this doctrine of "the indwelt God"; God resident within. And we know that that has often been seen and stressed in different ages under different names. We want that experience as taught in the New Testament, and any among us who feel they have it already, want more of it. So, we began yesterday on that quest and we began clean; washed in the blood of Christ. We loaded, as it were, the sludge ship with our sin—the gross and outward sins and the inward sins as well—nd, we are believing, now for holiness.

And now I want this morning to concentrate on two things. I want us to study how to covet, and then how to live what I call—forgive the phrase—the "we life." How to covet and how to live the "we life." This being, as I see it, [fundamental in order][3] to enter into the experience of having the mind of Christ in us.

Now our Lord said one day, "Beware of covetousness" [Luke 12:15]. And all through the New Testament there are warnings against covetousness.[4] Indeed those of you who are close Bible students may have noticed this strange thing that in the New Testament: covetousness and adultery are often linked together as such serious things. Nevertheless, though we are warned repeatedly in the New Testament against covetousness, I want us to learn today how to covet because it is quite mistaken to suppose that covetousness is always a sin.

---

1. The essence of this sermon was later published in *The Secret of Radiant Life* under the chapter titles "How to Covet" (ch. 25) and "How to Get 'We' in It" (ch. 26).

2. Missing on the recording.

3. Missing on the recording.

4. Also, Rom 1:20; 2 Cor 9:15; Eph 5:13; Col 3:5; 1 Thess 2:5; Heb 13:5; 2 Pet 2:3.

Covetousness is only a sin when it is directed to the wrong thing. Covetousness, so far from being a sin, is the very art of life when it is directed to to right things. Paul said, concluding that lesson that I read to you just now, "Covet earnestly the best gifts" [1 Cor 12:31]. So, let us learn how to covet.

Now, to covet an adequate income is a sensible thing. Who would ever covet an inadequate income? And yet, is that the best thing to covet? It would be better, would it not, to covet peace of mind? To covet health of body, that's a good thing. Whoever, that was sane, would covet sickness? And yet, to covet health of soul, that is a better thing, isn't it? Incomparably, the best thing of all to covet is this thing that we're considering in our morning sessions: God resident within; the "life of God in the soul of man";[5] God thinking, feeling, and willing in the heart of his consenting servant.[6] "Yet, I live no longer," says Paul, "but Christ liveth in me" [Gal 2:20]. Ah, that is undoubtedly the best thing of all, the greatest gift. If we can learn how to covet that, and receive it, then our task this week will be well on its way.

Now there are lots of people who would agree with me so far that it's right to covet the best gifts but they just don't know how to covet. They're not schooled in it. Coveting—the right kind of coveting—is both a science and an art. And that science and that art I want us to study now.

There are two major mistakes which even intelligent people are guilty in this matter of coveting. The first is this: that so many of them are vague, vague in the aim. They are not clear in mind as to what they are after, and unless you are clear in mind you can't covet. You know of the minister who was consulted on a spiritual problem one day by a young lady who was very smartly dressed and he said afterwards, "All vogue without, and all vague within." What a lot of people are vague within. We find that in ordinary ambition.

When I was a very young minister, there was a lad in my church who used to tell me whenever we talked how eager he was to get on. He was full of ambition. He meant to succeed. I've seldom met anybody who was so eager to succeed. But he was vague. He never pinpointed the aim. He never said, "I'm going for that, and after that, that." Never! He was always full of this yearning to succeed, which never, somehow or other, became concrete in its aim. It is many years since I left that church. I go back occasionally. He's still there. He's in middle life now, a little bent at the shoulders and bald. He's still talking about getting on. He's most eager to succeed—and he's still on the first rung of the ladder. One of his major faults was this: he had all the time remained vague in the aim. He will never arrive.

---

5. *The Life of God in the Soul of Man*, op. cit.
6. This type of mystical language is reminiscent of Scougal's emphases.

We will never arrive unless we are clear in the aim. It isn't even enough to say, "I want the mind of Christ." It isn't. I beg you receive this in the most reverent way that I am saying it: it isn't enough to look at our Lord and say, "I want to be like him." You must be more precise, more particular, more exact even than that. Where do you want to be like him? Do you know your major faults? Have you looked enough into the mirror of Christ to realise that self-centredness is your chief problem, that you are prone to jealousy, that you are proud? Do you know that you can see it all in the mirror of Jesus? Can you see the bias of your nature where most easily it runs to evil? Have you particularised the very opposite of that weakness and is that your aim, and is it clear and vivid in your mind? "I want the mind of Christ, and because I tend to pride, I long for his humility. I want to walk with him, humbly and in white."

In the same way that a boy in his early teens who finds himself all soft and undeveloped goes in for exercises because he wants a fit body and strong muscles. In the same way that some gawky girl has discovered that she can't walk with grace and would like to walk with grace. In the same way that she might go in for exercises by which she might learn how to walk with grace, so I beg you, be as plain about it as that. Particularise it. Don't be vague in your mind. "There is my weakness. I see its opposite in my Lord and that's the aim." I know it's a gift at the last; I know that. I know that at the last it won't be my achievement but his bestowal. But I'm fixing on the things I know I need. That first: no vagueness in the aim.

Here's the second thing: so many people who fail how to learn how to covet don't warm the object of their desires enough. It must be warm in the heart. You can't covet unless the thing is warm in the heart. Coveting is a strong word and when Paul used it in this phrase, "Covet earnestly the best gift; covet earnestly," he's making it as strong as he can. It's becoming obsessional with him. As we said yesterday, "Covet earnestly the best gift." To that clear aim must be added this warm, this passionate, this desiring heart. This: the mind of Christ, and those aspects of that mind I want above everything else. More and more it becomes the object of living to have his mind, and translate it in service to others.

I noticed—and there must be a reason for this; here I speak as an Englishman and you will have patience with me —I noticed that bicycles are not as common in America as they are in England. Maybe it's too hard work; I don't know. Or, maybe you fathers are very sensibly afraid of the traffic-infested streets and don't want your boys killed on a bicycle. But in England bicycles are common, and the passion of every little boy when he gets to a certain age is to get a bicycle. All of us, in turn, pass through that phase in England. And we study how to work on our fathers, and wear their resistance down, and get a bike. I want to show how to covet by asking you to picture a little English boy working on his dad to get a bike. He dreams of it every night; to have a bicycle of his own. He knows the one he wants. He knows the shop it's in. He goes and he presses his nose against the window until the point of his nose is a little round on the glass. And he stares at the bicycle. He knows everything about it. He knows how much dad must pay. Dad is still not worn down. Every bit of conversation in the home comes back to that bicycle. Mother says to him one day, "O son, don't you wear your shoes out quickly. I'm always taking them to the repairers." And the little boy says, "Yes, Mum, that's worrying me; all the money it's costing you to have my shoes repaired. I thought this, Mum; I thought this: 'If I had a bicycle I wouldn't have to walk to school. I'd ride and I wouldn't wear my shoes out.' You see, Mum." When he brings his report home from school at the end of term and hasn't done as well as his father thinks he ought, and dad has him in for an interview—the kind of interviews to which English boys get used at the end of every term—and when father tells him that it's not a good report from school and his place in the form is not as high as it should be, he says, "Dad, that's been worrying me. When I heard that I was only fifth in that form, I knew you were going to be upset, Dad. And Dad, it occurred to me if I had a bicycle and I could ride to school and ride home I'd save an hour every day, and then I'd work harder, Dad, at my homework and then my next report might be that I was top of the form." So he works on his father and mother. In the end he gets the bicycle. He does. They can't hold out against him. There's some kind of combination in nature that when the aim is clear and definite—as plain as a bicycle—and when your heart is longing for it like that, it has a way of coming.

Or, if I may take another domestic illustration: England is a poor country, in some ways, beside America. Washing machines are only just becoming common in England; indeed, they're not common yet. It's still something of a luxury. Oh, to have a washing machine! Imagine a working man's wife in England working on her husband to get a washing machine. Just as with the little boy, it keeps coming up in the conversation. She says to him, "You know, Dear, it will pain you to realise, there's always been a shadow on my happiness." And he says, "A shadow on your happiness, Lass? Why? We're happy together, aren't we?" She says, "Yes, but I always go to bed a little grim on Sunday night because I know tomorrow morning is washing day and I'll be standing over that tub all day Monday.[7] It's a kind of shadow on my happiness."

7. Whilst many US homes had some form of automated washing machine by the 1950s, in the UK washing machines did not become commonplace until the end of the 1950s. The economic fallout from WWII, including rationing, which was still in place in the UK until 1954, meant that the consumer market did not properly recover until the late 1950s and early 1960s.

He knows what's coming. She's round to the washing machine again. So she works at him, usually spread over many months in my country because he doesn't know where the money's coming from. But it happens in the end. In the end she gets a washing machine. You see, when the aim isn't vague; when it's clear—as plain as a washing machine; when you want it as much as that, it unlocks the difficulties and it arrives.

My dear friends, if that could be true in simple domestic things like a bicycle and a washer in England, how much more true is it in this deep truth that I am saying? Because, listen, when you are asking God to succeed in business you can't be absolutely sure that he wants you to, not absolutely sure. And when you are pleading with God for this advancement or that you can't be absolutely sure that that's his will. You don't know whether that's going to be for your advantage. It might be for your spiritual disadvantage. But when you want the mind of Christ you do know with every bit of you that that's what he wants you to want. And God's power always works to God ends. When you want that—when as clear as anything, "I want the mind of Christ; I want him dwelling in me now"—there's no doubt that you are in the line of his will and all the resources of heaven are moving with you and nothing can stop it, if only you will have that aim crystal clear; no vagueness here. If only you will keep it warm and passionate in your heart and hold it out to him—not just a vague feeling after a meeting in the auditorium, not something you have on Sunday but forget by Wednesday, but something you're living with all the time, that aim and longing—nothing can stop it. Not anything. It will be yours. So, I summarise this part of our discussion about how to covet by saying the major things to bear in mind all the time are: see that you have the objective clear in mind. See that you long for it ardently.

Now I know we run into what appears to be a psychological difficulty here. For some people will say at once—those of you who have followed me until now—"Ah, one moment preacher. Our feelings are not the slaves of our will. We can't be ardent just by wishing to be ardent, can we?" That's a good point, thank you! I must face it.

In my college days one of my friends fell violently in love. In my college days, in a Methodist college,[8] if you could help yourself it was best to keep out of love because we had to be celibate for seven years.[9] Only when they'd had

---

Before the arrival of automated washing machines it was somewhat of a tradition in the UK for Mondays to be washing days, with most of the day being devoted to the task. In Northern English industrial towns and cities the soapy water from the wash was used afterwards to clean the path and sidewalk in front of the house.

8. Sangster was at Handsworth College, Birmingham from early 1920 before being transferred to Richmond College, London in the summer. P. Sangster, *Doctor Sangster*, 48.

9. The original reasoning for this policy seems to have been, firstly, to test the calling

us for ministers for seven years would they allow us to marry. It seemed like fourteen years, but there it was. This friend of mine fell in love with a girl and every time he could escape the college he went to see her. This went on for some weeks and we all looked on with benign amusement. And then I think they had a little lovers' quarrel, and, came a weekend, and he didn't go out to see her. So we nailed a notice on his study door: "Out of Ardour!"

Ardour isn't the slave of the will, is it? When I said to you, "You must long for it passionately," those of you who were thinking with me were saying at once, "Ah, but can you do it? Can you do it? That's the whole trouble with our nature. It's one thing to know what you ought to covet, but Preacher it's another to thing to covet it. That's the bias of original sin in us. It's the wrong things that we covet so often. The right things we do not covet."

Let me say this to you then, meeting that difficulty, first, in regard to seeing it clearly: see yourself in the mirror of our Lord. Don't just say, "I want the mind of Christ." What aspects of the mind of the Christ do you most especially need? Particularise them. Be precise. "Here are my weaknesses. I know them. I have seen them in Jesus. I never saw myself till I saw myself in him. When I saw myself in him I saw myself for the first time. I saw the egotism, the thrustfulness of my nature. I saw the wrong things and, at the same time, in him, I saw their opposite. In my perfect Lord I saw what I wanted to be. I've got that precisely in mind." Now, warm that with desire. How does the longing for the life of Christ in those particulars become passionate?

Here it is. It will seem almost too simple to you to be convincing but I know it to be true: attend to those things. Just that! Attend to those things. Something's gone wrong with human nature, but originally we were made on the plan of God, and you were made to love these things! You were! And if you would only attend to them, ardour would arise in your soul for those very things. When you really see humility, pride stinks. When you really see selflessness, selfishness is the hateful and repugnant thing that it is. When you really see magnanimity, how it draws you. If you want ardour for these things, all you need do is to attend to them. Attend to them first in the life of your Lord; in the one who is all perfect and altogether lovely. First in him, and then

---

of the minister and, second, for financial reasons, as the church felt that they must take full responsibility for the upkeep of the whole minister's family, discouraging wives from working. The representative session of the 1955 British Methodist Conference passed a motion changing this, though the church was still even at this point hesitant in accepting married men into the ministry. "Agenda Representative Session 1955," 31. For an extensive discussion of British Methodism's engagement with preparation for ministry, probation and ordination during the twentieth century, see Brake, *Policy and Politics in British Methodism 1932–82*, 233–87.

after that, if you will allow me to add this word, for this has been the practice of half my lifetime, attend to them also in the lives of the saints.[10]

You see sometimes we say to ourselves, "Oh, Jesus was perfect, but then, he was God on earth. I can't be expected to be like that, can I?" But when you see the reflection of Jesus in his saints and see what he can do with our human nature, that objection is taken away from you. And you think, "If he could do that with Curé D'Ars;[11] if he could do that with Peter, with Augustine; if he could do that with Paul—he could do it with me!" He could, and you fix the aim. And you just attend to it, just attend to it, just attend to it. And the long- ing for it grows and grows, until it becomes obsessional. And then, and then, it's done. And then, it's done.

Are you struggling against a bad temper? See your Lord first, then see Fletcher of Madeley, that great Methodist saint.[12] Oh, oh what a man was Fletcher of Madeley. I wish he were better known among the Methodists in America.[13] There he was, a fiery, a fiery young army officer: a word and a blow!

10. Sangster's book *The Pure In Heart* demonstrates the breadth of his engagement with "the saints" of all traditions.

11. See n. 138[**X-REF**], below.

12. John William Fletcher (1729–85), Church of England minister, born in Switzer- land with the original name Jean Guillaume de la Fléchère. Following a very short time in the army he came to England in 1750 and became tutor to the sons of Thomas Hill, a Shropshire MP. Fletcher was converted in 1755 and was inducted as vicar in Madeley in 1760, with his ministry being known for its preaching and pastoral qualities, at a time of the advent of the Industrial Revolution. Indeed, Madeley was within a key coal mining and iron producing area. He also developed a wider ministry, but rejected itineracy as proposed and propagated by John Wesley. In fact, Fletcher envisaged Methodism only within the Church of England. Fletcher became a key interpreter of Methodist theology in the eighteenth century, and one of Methodism's first great theologians, developing a distinct Dispensational model, strongly Arminian in emphasis. Recent studies of Fletcher and his wife are focusing on Fletcher's attempts to pursue a distinct model of Methodism fully integrated within the Church of England parochial system (David Wilson, 2010). Fletcher's early death from typhoid frustrated John Wesley's plans for Fletcher to become his nominated successor. Forsaith, "Fletcher, John William (1729–1785)."

13. While it is difficult with any certainty to establish the evidence Sangster had for this comment, or whether he is referring to scholarship or a general knowledge within US congregations, twentieth- and twenty-first-century Methodist scholarship in the US has certainly had a tendency to have a primary focus on John Wesley, and to a lesser extent on Charles Wesley, perhaps to the neglect of other figures. Only one significant piece of research had been conducted on Fletcher prior to Sangster's comment, interestingly in the US: Shipley, "Methodist Arminianism in the Theology of John Fletcher" (1942). Before 1956 most British engagements with Fletcher were non-academic and more biographical. Indeed it seems from Sangster's own writings that he is reliant on two sources: Tyerman, *Wesley's Designated Successor* (1882) and the original article from *Encyclopedia Britan- nica*, 11th ed., 10:498. George Lawton produced two articles shortly before and after the WMC 1956: "Madeley in the Eighteenth Century," and "John Fletcher's Incumbency at

And then he came to Christ.[14] And then he coveted the mind of Christ. And then he received it. And he became almost a legend. People behind his back called him "the Seraphic Fletcher."[15] His dear wife said of him, "I have lived with an angel."[16] And that just wasn't wifely bias. That was the very truth of it. Robert Southey,[17]—who was no Methodist at all, who was opposed to Methodism in part—it was Robert Southey himself who said, "No church had a more apostolic figure than the Methodists had in John Fletcher of Madeley."[18] His bad temper, gone. Is pride your sin, unconsciously maybe? Oh, it's often unconscious. Believe me, getting rid of pride is like peeling an onion; every skin you take off there's another skin underneath.

Is pride your besetting sin? Then read the life of Curé d'Ars.[19] How ever did he get through college, I don't know. They were so short of priests in the early years of the eighteenth century in France that they had to take in some

---

Madeley," however, there is no evidence that these informed Sangster either here or in his later printed works. Contemporary research on Fletcher has been, for the most part, conducted by British scholars or through British universities.

14. Born into privilege, he attended Geneva University (1746) but rejected the ministry to pursue a military career, travelled to Lisbon and enlisted in the army. An accident prevented him from sailing with his regiment to Brazil. Forsaith, "Fletcher, John William (1729–1785)."

15. Tyerman quotes Robert Hall as having said, "Fletcher is a seraph who burns with the ardour of divine love." Tyerman, *Wesley's Designated Successor*, v.

16. See Tyerman, *Wesley's Designated Successor*, 473, 561–65.

17. This information seems to be derive from Tyerman's account.
Robert Southey (1774–1843), English poet and reviewer and poet laureate (1813). Probably best known for his *Life of Nelson* (1813). He wrote during a time of social and political instability and fought for and defended the establishment in his writings. In particular he wrote strongly worded texts in support of the Church of England, supporting the laws excluded Roman Catholics from public office and Parliament. Southey published *The Book of the Church* (1824), a history of Christianity in England, which celebrated the established church "which had shown itself the guardian of religious and political liberty." The book was not received without controversy. *Vindiciae ecclesiae Anglicanae* (1826) was Southey's response, making the political significance of the Church of England explicit. Carnall, "Southey, Robert (1774–1843)," *ODNB*.

18. Taken from Tyerman, *Wesley's Designated Successor*, v–vi.

19. Jean Baptiste Marie Vianney (1786–1859). He received little formal education, perhaps due to the uncertain times during the French Revolution. He became a cattle hand. Vianney struggled with Latin during his seminary training but was allowed into the Catholic priesthood due to his common sense and goodness. From 1818 he ministered as priest in Ars-en-Dombes, where he became renowned for his sanctity. His ability to read hearts led him to becoming a sought-after confessor. People came in the thousands to the small village to receive confession. He was beatified on Jan 5, 1905 and canonised on May 31, 1925. See Casey, "Vianney, Jean Baptiste Marie, St." Sangster seems to have been reliant on Ghéon, *Secret of the Curé D'Ars*.

men that really didn't make the grade, and among them they took in this little man, John Vianney, who is known to all the world now as the Curé d'Ars.

When the bishop came to the college to decide who should be ordained the professors took his name off the list. They said, "There's one man, my Lord, you can't ordain. He's a very devoted man. And he spends much time in prayer, but ha! Ha! But he really hasn't mastered the curriculum."

"What's his name?" said the bishop.

"John Vianney."

"Oh, did you say he was much in prayer?"

"Oh yes, my Lord, that's part of his trouble. He neglects his studies to pray."

The bishop said, to the astonishment of the professors, "I'll ordain him!" And they said, "No, no, no, my Lord. We don't . . ."

He said, "I'll ordain him!"[20]

And so, he was snipped into the ministry like that. Pulled in, almost by the hair of his head. And he became the greatest priest in France and all people spiritually sensitive went to the place he transformed. They sent him to a little village where he couldn't do much harm. And there began a ten-years fight in that village between heaven and hell. And then at the end heaven won. All the dance halls and all the pubs folded up. He didn't preach against them. They just folded up. Somebody came down from Paris and said to man from Ars, "What wonderful people you are here." And the man from Ars, who was an honest man, said to the man from Paris, he said, "We're not really, but there are some things you can't do when there's a saint about."[21] He had the mind of Christ. Christ was born again in him. This thing we are seeking, it was true in that little priest.

But it was his humility I wanted to tell you of. Listen, my dear friends, when a man succeeds like that he can excite the envy of his other ministerial breather. Alas, and the Curé D'Ars did and the priests in all the villages and towns round about took a dislike to him because his church was packed and everybody was streaming to see this man. And they remembered what a poor scholar he was when he was at college. And you know, they got up a round robin. Do you know what a round robin is? Do you use them here? A document, and everybody signs in a circle so nobody knows afterwards who started it. They got up a round robin and sent it to the bishop, beseeching him to unfrock this little priest because of his ignorance of theology. And just before it was sent to the bishop, either by mistake or bravado—that question has never

20. Ghéon, *Secret of the Curé D'Ars*, 32.

21. Ghéon, *Secret of the Curé D'Ars* relates numerous stories of how Jean Vianney was recognised widely within France as a saint even in his lifetime.

been cleared up—it was sent to the little Curé himself. He read it all: all the criticisms about himself, all it had to say about his ignorance and enthusiasm. He read it all, and he read it again. And he agreed with it all. He agreed with it. He agreed with it. And when the round robin arrived on the bishop's desk, his own name was there as well.[22] He joined himself with his accusers in inviting a condemnation which he agreed with them in believing he deserved. When you see humility like that—you see it again; this is the mind of Jesus. Here is another incarnation of our blessed Lord's Spirit in frail human flesh. It is all of grace, every bit of it. The Curé knew that better than anyone.

My friends, here's a suggestion: after your Bible, a Word of God first, you read some of the lives of the saints. Sometimes put your novel down. I'm not shutting you out from all novels but sometimes put your novel down and read a life of one of the saints. At least it will be true! And when you turn the last page there will be a longing in you, there will. You will again have seen the Spirit of Jesus incarnate in human flesh and this prayer will be flaming in your heart, "Do it again. Lord, do it again. Do it in me." So, you are learning to covet. The aim crystal clear, the longing passionate and increasing, a clear understanding that it's not a human achievement but a gift of God. But an opening, and an opening, and an opening, of your nature and then that ardent desire of what Charles Wesley said in one of his hymns:

Drawn by the lure of strong desire
O come and consecrate my breast.[23]

And drawn by the lure of strong desire, he'll come and consecrate your breast. And being humble, as you will be, you won't know it's happening. We'll know. We'll know. For those of us who see you, those who live with you, your folk at church or where you work, they'll say, "She grows more and more luminous. She seems to be more magnanimous, more humble than ever." You're beautifully unaware of it.[24] They see God.

By one of the most glorious subtleties of Providence, has seen to it that the more we possess in holiness, the lower we think in our own esteem. And here's the way it happens: the nearer you come to the eternal throne and to the

22. Ghéon, *Secret of the Curé D'Ars*, 128–29.

23. The third and fourth lines of the first stanza of Charles Wesley's hymn "Come, Holy Ghost, All-Quick'ning Fire," in *CHPCM*, 532–33.

24. One of Sangster's strongest critiques of John Wesley's understanding of Christian holiness was against the emphasis upon the assurance of having been made holy and Wesley's admonition to testify to being entirely sanctified. Sangster's position suggests a correlation between the attainment of holiness and a corresponding feeling of unworthiness; the saint will not know of their own holiness. For a full discussion of Sangster's critique, see Cheatle, *W. E. Sangster – Herald of Holiness*, 143–48.

burning holiness of God, the more aware are you of the stains that do remain on yourself. And so the higher you rise actually, the lower you sink in your own estimation. So, you won't know, but others will. And your power, and your influence and your usefulness to God, oh how mighty. The mighty people of the earth are the saints of God in whom Jesus dwells. You must know that. The world's great men are often little men. The Alexanders, and the Caesars, and the Napoleons. What in the ages do they matter? Those who matter are the saints of God. They shape the ages. In heaven you will see how true this is.

My friends, time flies fast in Junaluska, and I will steal another moment or two, if you'll allow me, to deal with the second thing I promised. I said, first, we'd discover how to covet, how important it is to covet; the precise aim, the passionate desire, the way to it, the how to.

And, now more briefly, how to live the "we life." We want the mind of Christ. We want him living in us. Ultimately we want to be where St. Paul was when he could say, "I live; yet no longer I, but Christ liveth in me" [Gal 2:20]. But at this stage we'll do it together. We'll live the "we life."

We tell a story in England about a village organist who was very proud of his instrument, and with less justice proud of his ability in playing it. It was an old fashioned instrument. It wasn't blown by electricity. It had to be pumped behind. And the village half-wit used to sit behind a curtain pumping the wind in it. So the village organist, one weekday evening, was giving a recital. The people who had come were very appreciative and every little while he got up from the organ stool and bowed to their applause and he went back and he said, "And now I will play you something else." And when he had done that about eight times—"Now I will play you something else"—he put his fingers on the keys and no sound came, not any. There was an embarrassed silence. There was no wind in the instrument. And then the cowled[25] head of the half-wit appeared from the little curtain behind and he said rebukingly to the organist, "Let's have a little more 'we' in this." "Let's have a little more 'we' in this." He wanted it to be understood that he was doing his part as well. It wasn't a solo performance. That there were two of them at it. That's why he said, "Let's have a little more 'we' in it."

My dear friends, in this life, in this Christian life, this deeper life, we want to get more "we" in it. One of the reasons why some of us are failing so seriously is that there's too much "I" in it. We want to live the "we life." When we read the Word of God and read it in the book of Acts of the Apostles, we come on occasion to certain passages that we call the "we" passages. We will all have noticed them. We think the book was written by Luke, Paul's friend and physician. In most of the book he's writing in the third person; "They did this.

25. Hooded.

They did that." But there are passages, and one classic passage in particular, where he says, "We went." "*We* did." "*We! We!*" And, it's obvious he was in the party at that time and he writes with more particularity and more detail. You could almost see St. Luke with his journal, with his journal, his diary at his side reminding himself of precisely what happened on that occasion and is writing it into the record. We call those—which my ministerial brethren will remember well—the "we" passages. We need more "we" passages in our book of life. If we are to reach that point where Christ lives in us one necessary stage on the way is to live the "we life."

How are we to make this real? We want his mind in ours. And we saw yesterday that the transference of one mind to another seems mystical and difficult. But one way—in a sense, the only way we this can work—is that we are all the time beholden him in our minds. "We." "We"—to live, mentally, in our Lord.

And one simple way of doing it is, I say, if you are not already doing it—and my dear friend Dr. Frank Laubach has been practicing it for years; I learned that in conversation with him this morning—before you begin your day and come to consciousness, begin to talk with him under your breath. "We have a full day before us, Lord. We shall have difficulties to face, Lord. We shall have opportunities, Lord, Lord." "*We! We! We!*" "We must make the most of this day, Lord." If it sounds slightly irreverent to some of you, does it? If you think so, I'm telling you this: the saints of God through the ages, though they haven't often spoken that way, they have practiced this thing. And in part they talked like that with him and they learned the "we life."

At the end of the day review your day. Go over it backwards. There is a psychological reason why it's better to go over the day backwards. And if you go talk with him, still, "We were able to do that Lord." "We left a blessing there Lord." "Some of them were helped by us, weren't they, Lord?" But every now and then you'll come to something where your speaking alone; something you did on your own and something you didn't do well. And then you will find yourself saying, "I did that myself, Lord. That's why it went wrong. In success we succeeded. In failure I failed alone." Now the more you take him in your life, in the conversations of the soul—and remember the most important conversations you have they are not with other people; they are with Jesus. They're always the more important conversations. Remember that we do most of our living within. This is the important part. So talk with him and you will realise increasingly as time goes by that you are of course very much the junior partner in it. But you are a partner, a partner. And he allows you to say "we." "We."

You've all heard, I judge, the fable, the old fable we used to tell, about the elephant and a mouse who once walked over a wooden bridge together. And when they got to the further side the mouse said to the elephant, "We made that bridge shake, didn't we?"[26]

You will feel, "Oh, my part in this, Lord, is so small." But the more he comes in, the more he controls, the nearer you will come to having the mind that was in Christ.

O Lord, we are all unworthy.
More love to thee, O Christ.
More love to thee.
Help us for thy love's sake.
Amen.

---

26. This story can be traced back to a cartoon strip by Ed Kuekes, *Cleveland Plain Dealer*, May 17, 1936, 10.

CHAPTER 5

How to Make a Name

To him that overcometh I will give a new name, a new name.[1]

WHEN I CAME INTO the auditorium last evening I was struck by the youth of the company. Maybe I was looking mainly at the choir at first. But I thought, "What a magnificent group of young people." When I stood up to address the whole company I could still see the youth were prominently here. Mark you, I am glad it's not all youth. I think this segregation of the age groups in religious assemblies can be overdone. I think that age needs the enthusiasm of youth and youth needs the experience of age, and it is the will of God that we do his work together. But as I looked at those young people, this thought dropped into my mind: "You must tell them sometime, during this week how, to make a name, how to make a name."

All normal young people desire to make a name. They may be so modest that they have no hope of making a name that shall reverberate round all the world, or be known in all the nation, but every normal person likes to be known where they're known; in the town, in their own circle. The ache for at least a little bit of fame is in us all. If you don't think that's true of you, if you feel a slight sense of superiority now, just you remember your feeling when you are being introduced to somebody four times and they still didn't know you. You went away afterwards saying to yourself, "Is my personality so unimpressive that I didn't make any mark on his mind at all?" Then you will know that even you desire to be known. You want in some small way, at least, to make a name.

Some people say, "But what's a name? Names don't matter!" Shakespeare said it on one great occasion, we recall. He said, "What's in a name? A rose by any other name would smell as sweet."[2] And yet, there is a good deal in a

---

1. Paraphrase of Rev 2:17.
2. Shakespeare, *Romeo and Juliet*, act 2, scene 2, line 48.

name. They know it in business. Oh yes they do. The fishermen, the trawler-men who reap the silver harvest of the sea round my island home, they catch a fish which they call "dogfish." But when it gets to the fishmonger's for sale, it is no longer called dogfish. It's the same fish, but the man that has to sell it calls it "rock salmon." Believe me, it's more rock than salmon.

Both in England and America we know "artificial silk," but they've got a better name for artificial silk now. On both sides of the Atlantic, they call it "rayon." In England and in American we both know what a bookmaker is. He's busy in both countries plying his dubious trade. Now, I don't know if they're doing it in America, but in England they're no longer calling them-selves "bookmakers." Oh no, they've got a better name. They call themselves now "turf accountants." He's still the same old bookie. He is.

Most people have at least two names. There is an exception even to that rule. There is a man—where is that man?—in America, of course, who only has one name. You see when he was born, a good many years ago now, his mother and father couldn't agree on what his first name, his Christian name, should be. So they said, "We won't give him one. We'll let him grow up and choose the one he likes." When he grew up he decided it was more distinctive not to have a Christian name at all. So he goes through life with one name. I've seen the entry in the telephone directory. It's there as well. If he came to live in England we'd take him for a lord, because in England only a lord can sign his letters just by his name. McIntosh. The McIntosh. The McIntosh of McIntoshes. *The McIntosh* —nothing else. If I had time this evening and wasn't bent on a high spiritual purpose, I could so gladly have discussed with you the origin of names, for they're interesting and they've interested me a long time.

Many girls' Christian names are taken, as you know, from flowers, so appropriately: Daisy and Lily and Rose. There is only one boy's name taken from flowers, and it isn't George, [Dr. Kerry],[3] and it isn't Frank, Dr. Laubach. Modesty forbids me. They knew what it is, but even my modesty can't prevent me from helping the intelligent among you in remembering that it's William. In the old says our forebears were glad for the most part to get the names for their children from the Word of God. What better place for them? But in more recent years people are happy not to use those of the Holy Word. They've been going to Holywood for names. And I don't admire some of their choices.

Oh, if I had time I would discuss with you the origins of those surnames among you that stem down from England: the names that were taken from occupations like Smith and Butcher and Brewer and Butler; and those that came from relationships like Johnson, the son of John; and Wilson, the son of

3. The name is unclear; either Kelly, Carey or Kerry. The *Proceedings* of the conference give no names that aid with identifying further to whom Sangster is referring.

Will; and from relationships once removed like Dickinson, the son of the king of Dick; and Tomlinson, the son of the king of Tom; or those names that were taken in my country from localities and which I meet so often in America too, like Ridge and Hill and Wood and Dale; and those names also that were originally nicknames, turned into proper surnames, like Hunter and Drinkwater and Golightly; and that most famous of all names, Shakespeare, for that began as a nickname and has become a name of enormous renown.

O my dear friends, if I were lecturing, if we were here mainly for interest and a little sun, I'd be glad to talk on those things and invite you to lie if you wish and to say, "My name is so and so. What is it's derivation, if you know it?" But I have a spiritual purpose in mind. I want to tell you, I want to tell the young people especially, how to make a name. And into that I'll expand now.

I always remember the night I heard the phrase "making a name." My father used it to my mother. I was a boy at home and laying the supper table. Father was reading the paper and he put it down and said to mother, "This young fellow, Smith, is making a name? Never mind who the "Smith" was, but father was right. He made a name: F. E. Smith, [Garather Smith], they called him, First Earl of Birkenhead, Lord Chancellor of England.[4] Father was right; he made a name.

But I fell to wondering as a boy, what is it to make a name? What is it to make a name? I'm going to give you the key this evening. Take this to heart, you young people especially. And you senior people, you check me as I go, and see if your minds mark with mine. And will you agree with me when I say this? You must always be careful, first, where you want to make the name. The rules vary according to where you want to make the name. If you want to make a name on earth, I'll give you the rules. I'll give you those rules [for above][5] also, but they are not parallel and that distinction must be borne in mind all the time.

---

4. Frederick Edwin Smith (1876–1970), British lawyer and politician, renowned for his sharp mind, eloquent tongue and wit. Made an enormous impact on entering Parliament with his maiden speech on March 12, 1906, being termed "one of the most celebrated débuts in parliamentary history—a masterpiece of impudent satire which made him a star overnight." *Hansard* 4, 153, March 12, 1906, 1014–23. As a young lawyer he quickly built a brilliant reputation representing some of the biggest companies and names in the UK. He became lord chancellor, head of the judiciary, by age forty-six. He took the title Lord Birkenhead (February 3, 1919). His most important act as lord chancellor, however, was probably his part in the signing of the treaty which created the Free State of Ireland in December 1921. Campbell, "Smith, Frederick Edwin, First Earl of Birkenhead (1872–1930)," *ODNB*.

5. This is either missed out unintentionally by Sangster or the tape is damaged and misses this out.

You can make a name on earth about anything. You can. You can make a name on earth about anything. You can make it out of crime: John Dillinger[6] and Al Capone,[7] they made a name. We all know that you can make a name out of crime.

You can make a name out of literature. Do you know Doctor Bowdler by name?[8] Doctor Bowdler, years ago, came to the conclusion that Shakespeare wasn't quite fit for children to read. And so, he went all through Shakespeare's plays and took out the parts that he didn't think were quite fit for the children. And we turned his name into a verb. And any volume that is expurgated like that, we say it's been "bowdlerised." So, he made name.

You all know the name of Captain Boycott,[9] an Englishman who had his place in Ireland and he fell out with his tenants. And they made a pact among themselves that they would never work for him, not any of them. "We won't work for him." And they didn't. And everyone knows what a boycott is now.

6. John Dillinger (1903–34) was American criminal and bank robber.

7. Alphonse Gabriel Capone (1899–1947) was a notorious American gangland boss, aspects of whose life is portrayed in numerous films and TV series.

8. Thomas Bowdler (1754–1825), English writer and literary editor who became immortalised by his strict moral editing of Shakespeare's works. In 1807, together with his sister he produced the first version of *The Family Shakespeare*, a version that he felt suitable for children. Neither the first edition or the 1818 edition occasioned offense. In 1821, however, an edition of *Blackwood's Magazine* rounded on Bowdler's version. Lord Jeffrey posted a defense of Bowdler in the *Edinburgh Review* and "went so far as to state that all other editions of Shakespeare had been rendered obsolete." According to Clare Loughlin-Chow, "*The Family Shakspeare* ran into many editions, more importantly it affected how Shakespeare was edited and read for generations." Loughlin-Chow, "Bowdler, Thomas (1754–1825)," *ODNB*.

9. Charles Cunningham Boycott (1832–97), land agent renowned for his unsympathetic treatment of Irish tenants. In 1873 he became agent for Lord Erne, who owned huge tracks of land in Co. Mayo, Ireland. The unfair rents imposed by Erne, through boycott led to a laborers' revolt, who refused to work for him, and isolated him from contact with the wider community, making it exceptionally difficult to obtain provisions from the neighbouring Irish population. He was verbally abused and spat at. The Irish also managed to practically blockade the postal service to his address. The word "boycott" first came into parlance in 1880. According to Anne Pimlott Baker, the term was used in capitals in the *Daily News* of December 13, 1880. It came into more general use to describe measures used to isolate an institution or a country. Norgate, "Boycott, Charles Cunningham (1832–97)." Baker, "Charles Cunningham Boycott (1832–97)," *ODNB*.

The Earl of Cardigan[10] made a name, commander of our armies in the Crimean War.[11] In the fierce cold of that Russian winter he got somebody to knit him a woollen waistcoat. And I heard a girl speaking today about her cardigan sweater. And she didn't know that she was returning, I think, to the noble Earl who made a name. The man that made a raincoat made a name. We all know what a Mackintosh is.[12]

I had a sandwich for lunch today, a nice one. The Earl of Sandwich[13] gave his name to that. You see, he was a great gambler. He was such a gambler he wouldn't leave the table, not even to eat. And when the waiter came and said to him one day, "My Lord, your meal is waiting," he said, "I can't come to the dining room for it. Get a piece of bread, get a piece of meat and put it on top; get another piece of bread and put in on top. Then bring it to me." And that is how the sandwich got invented. People said, "What a funny way of eating." So, they took the gambler's name, the Earl of Sandwich, and we've all been eating sandwiches since, without realising who you were following.

I say, isn't it odd the way you can make a name on earth? You can make it any way. You can make it by crime. You can make it by garments. You can make it by work. You can make it by folly? Why should the name of the man that made a raincoat be remembered and the man that invented the wheel be forgotten? Why should gamblers be recalled through the centuries and many

10. James Brudenell, seventh Earl of Cardigan (1797–1868), British army officer who became famous for his exploits in the Crimean War (1853–56), leading bravely, though perhaps foolishly, the "charge of the light brigade" during the Battle of Balaclava (October 25, 1854). The garment that became synonymous his name is supposedly to have been modelled after the knitted woollen waistecoats that British officers had made to cope with the severe winter weather of Crimea. The folklore about the "charge of the light brigade" and the fame that Lord Cardigan achieved on returning to England as a hero led to the rise of the garment's popularity. Sweetman, "Brudenell, James Thomas, Seventh Earl of Cardigan (1797–1868)," *ODNB*. Also see David, *Homicidal Earl*, 431–36.

11. The Crimean War (1853–56), a conflict between Britain, France, the Ottoman Empire and Sardinia against Russia.

12. Charles Macintosh (1766–1843), Scottish manufacturing chemist and inventor of waterproof fabrics that carry his name. In a celebrated legal case in 1836 about the infringement of his waterproofing patent by a London firm of silk manufacturers, Everington & Son, in which the jury vindicated his invention and his name then passed almost immediately into English parlance. Prosser, "Macintosh, Charles (1766–1843)," *ODNB*.

13. John Montagu (1718–92), fourth Earl of Sandwich, First Lord of the Admiralty. Sangster's reference to his gambling seems to be part of folklore rather than fact. According Rodger, one of his biographers, he did "not appear to have been much of a gambler, though it was the vice of the age, and he continued to live frugally, but he began to acquire the reputation of libertine which has never left him." Whatever the case, his name is now universally associated with slices of bread with filling in between. See "Sandwich Celebrates 250th Anniversary of the sandwich." Also see Rodger, "Montagu, John, Fourth Earl of Sandwich (1718–1792)," *ODNB*.

an obscure saint of God be forgotten? Why? Because, there is something freakish and bizarre and stupid in the way that you can make a name on earth.

But there is nothing freakish or bizarre or stupid about the way you make a name in heaven. Listen. Listen again to the Word of God. God said, "To him that overcometh I will give a new name; a new name to him that overcometh."[14] "Overcometh" what? The world and the flesh and the devil. The deep selfishness in all our nature, the shutting of our eyes and our ears to the cry of the suffering world that we have been reminded about so much by Doctor Laubach in these recent days. Those living just for themselves—"Just for me." Or, if you will keep the grace of God to conquer that; to learn how to live on your own circumference, and have Christ at the very centre of your life. If you will overcome by "the Overcomer," God says, "I will give you a new name. I will give you a new name."

I wonder how many of you here know the name of Henry Martyn?[15] When I tell you that he was judged by some people to be the most heroic figure in the English church in four hundred years? I think that a slight exaggeration, but many people judged him so to be: the most heroic figure in the English church in four hundred years. You will have some input in the name even though you're hearing it for the first time. He was born and grew up in Cornwall, our western-most county. His mother died when he was young. He was a poor, inferior little boy. He had warts on his face. And with the cruelty of schoolboys, his companions made fun of him. He wasn't on the games. He couldn't join in their games. He used to play in the corner of the playground, shunned and peered at. There was only one thing that was strange about him: he had a marvelous brain. They discovered that early at school. It was like a sponge. It could draw up everything they put it on, everything. Scholarships, how he took them. He got to our University of Cambridge by scholarship and in those days it was almost a miracle to do it. And he was Senior Wrangler before he was twenty-one; the highest distinction in mathematics. [Not anybody could win].[16] And they couldn't believe that a boy less than twenty-one had done it. Smith's Prizeman, Fellow of St. John's, the distinctions, the gold medals—fell just into his lap. The only thing his professors couldn't understand was whether he was greater at mathematics or greater at languages. You see, when he was tired with maths at the end of the day he didn't pick up a novel as I might do, or you, to rest his mind. No, when he was tired with

---

14. A paraphrase and partial repetition of Rev 2:17.

15. Henry Martyn (1781–1812). Sangster seems to have utilised Padwick's biography of Martyn, *Henry Martyn: Confessor of the Faith*, for his account: Also see Bennett, "Martyn, Henry."

16. Inaudible.

maths he would pick up a Persian grammar, and have a lovely hour resting his mind with a Persian grammar. What a man! We intended—that was the subject of their discussion—what a name he'll make, what a name! He will make a name in half a dozen callings. And people wondered what will happen to Henry Martyn. Then it happened: he met Jesus Christ one day. And Jesus said, "Can you give me your heart? Give me all of you, your mind as well?" And Henry said, "Take it, Lord. What wilt thou have me to do?" And the Lord said, "Henry, go to India. Go as a missionary. My people in India need the Word of God. Go and give it to them." And Henry said, "Yes, Lord, I go." And, then something else happened. After he said "Yes" to God, for the first time, the only time in his life, he fell in love with a girl, named Lydia. He said, "Lydia, I am going to India as a missionary. Come with me." And she said, "Henry, I'll marry you but I won't go to India. You stay here and I'll marry you." And the great sacrifice of his life and how he suffered in his brain: "India or Lydia? India or Lydia?" He chose the right. He went to India and he went alone.[17] The rest of the story is history—that amazing brain. He remains still the prince of translators. Although Doctor Laubach ought to be giving an opinion about this, I doubt, I doubt anybody has paralleled his amazing achievements in so short a time. He turned that phenomenal brain to the translation of the Scriptures. First, the New Testament into Hindustani, into Arabic, Persian, one after the other, he did. And on his way home for a brief furlough he died in Tokat, in Asia Minor, without a fellow countryman anywhere near him to hear his last wishes, or to say "Amen" to his last prayers. Dead! Dead at thirty-one! The task finished! It is done, Lord. Into Hindustani, into Persian, into Arabic. What do you suggest the professors at Cambridge said as he went as a missionary? "Of all the wastes, of all the things he might have done." He could have had nationally, maybe internationally undying fame in his own lifetime. He gave all he had to Christ and his fame is secure forever in heaven.

Oh yes, you grand young people, you can make a name on earth by anything, by anything. If you want to make a name in heaven you must be [availed][18] to overcome.

And here is the second piece of counsel to you: if you are going to make a name on earth you've got, you young folk—somehow or other, you've got to do it—you've got to constantly be making it in the papers, and on the radio, and you have to appear quite often in TV, on TV. You must. You see those are the great organs, so they say, of public knowledge. And if you are to come to fame, this is the way you must do it: into the press, onto the radio,

---

17. Martyn was travelling home on furlough with an aim of pursuing his lost love when he became ill and later died. Padwick, *Henry Martyn*, 177–80.

18. Unclear.

and onto TV. That's how the man on the street judges fame; whether he's heard of you.

I heard two men, two men talking on a bus in London the other evening. One of them mentioned a name and his friend said, "Never heard of him!" So, he said the name again and his friend said, "Yes, I heard you. Never heard of him!" And he said it in such a way to imply that if he'd never heard of him he wasn't worth hearing about. That's the judgement of the world. Nothing so describes the sense of values on this earth than the people who are known and the people who are not known.

You all know this . . . lady that turned up in London the other day, named—I think I may have got it wrong; I'm not expert in these things. If the name was Monroe or something like that—Marilyn Monroe.[19] The choir know all of these things. Marilyn Monroe, that's it. You all know Rita Hayworth.[20] You all know Ava Gardner, yes![21] These distinguished women, drifting from one husband to another.[22] You know them! But how many in the world, or for that matter in this auditorium this evening, how many know of Semmelweis,[23] the man that discovered the secret of the dreadful Childbed Fever and made it possible for our mothers to have their babies in safety? How many here even know the name of George Minot, the man that discovered the liver cure for pernicious anaemia?[24] How many of you know the man I sat with for twelve

19. Marilyn Monroe (1926–62), original name Norma Jean Mortenson, was a famous American actress, singer, model and sex symbol. Spoto, *Marilyn Monroe*.

20. Rita Hayworth (1918–87), original name Margarita Carmen Cansino, a famous American actress and dancer, the peak of whose career was mainly in the mid-1940s. Leaming, *If This Was Happiness*.

21. Ava Gardner (1922–90), American actress and singer whose acting career continued until the mid-1980s. She had a number of high-profile relationships, including wiht Howard Hughes and Frank Sinatra. Server, *Ava Gardner*.

22. At the time of this sermon Monroe had just started her third marriage, Hayworth had just ended her fourth marriage and Gardner was in her third marriage.

23. Ignaz Philipp Semmelweis (1818–65), Hungarian physician and early pioneer of antiseptic procedures, famed for discovering that the occurrences of the often-fatal "childbed fever" (puerperal fever) could be drastically reduced by proper hand cleansing. Later given the title of "prophet of bacteriology." Hanninen et al., "Ignaz Philipp Semmelweis."

24. George Minot (1885–1950), American Nobel Prize winner, who with George Hoyt Whipple and William P. Murphy discovered a treatment for the then-fatal disease pernicious anemia. In an interesting twist of fate, with particular reference to this collections of sermons, Minot, himself a diabetic, was treated for diabetes as a result of the work of Frederick Banting and Charles Best's discovery of insulin in 1921. So, by the benefit of one treatment, which kept Minot alive, another life-changing discovery and cure could be made. Rackemann, *Inquisitive Physician*; Castle "Gordon Wilson Lecture: A Century of Curiosity about Pernicious Anemia."

years on the senate of my university, Sir Ambrose Flemming,[25] who discovered penicillin?[26] Sir Ambrose Flemming on this side of me, and Sir Robert Watson Watt[27] on that side, the man who invented radar. Not bad company to keep was it? Though I fear I let it down a bit myself.

All these are not the well-known names. No. The world judges worth another way. I'm telling you, if you want to make a name on earth: into the papers, onto the films, onto radio, and then to TV. I have no criticism of the best of our newspapers. God forbid. On the whole I have been kindly treated by the press. But I have often thought that editors exaggerate their own importance in the community. And, if I could illustrate what I mean I would take the editor of a religious newspaper which will be known by many, all my ministerial brethren here: the *British Weekly*, because, though it's published in England it has a circulation beyond England. Its famous editor of a generation ago is a man named Robertson Nicoll.[28] Oh, how keen he was to get people to write

25. Sangster has confused the name of Sir Ambrose Fleming (1849–1945), an electrical engineer and researcher, with Sir Alexander Fleming, the bacteriologist. Sangster was first elected to the senate of London University in 1944 and served for twelve year, so his time overlaps with that of Sir Alexander Fleming.

26. Sir Alexander Fleming (1881–1955), medical researcher and Nobel Prize winner, with Howards Florey and Ernst Boris Chain, for the discovery of the antibiotic fungi Penicillium notatum in 1928. Sir Alexander Fleming remains one of the best-known British scientists of the twentieth century. McIntyre, "Alexander Fleming (1881–1955)"; Worboys, "Fleming, Sir Alexander (1881–1955)," *ODNB*.

27. Sir Robert Alexander Watson-Watt (1892–1973), Scottish scientist and developer of radar. Having developed a cathode ray direction finder for the navy in the 1920s, Watson-Watt, with the growing menace of Nazi Germany, was commissioned to find out a way of stopping bombers. In February 1935 Watson-Watt submitted a draft proposal for utilising radio waves as a means of detection, *The Detection of Aircraft by Radio Methods*. He called this RADAR (Radio Detection and Ranging). A trial with an aircraft was successful and three years before the outbreak of WWII Watson-Watt became superintendent of Bawdsey Research Station, near Felixstowe. By early 1940 these small beginnings led to the establishment of a wide-ranging defense system for southern England, which arguably kept Britain from defeat. Radar is now ubiquitous. Jones, "Watt, Sir Robert Alexander Watson-Watt (1892–1973)," *ODNB*. His own account of the invention can be found in Watson-Watt, *Three Steps to Victory*.

28. Sir William Roberston Nicoll (1851–1923), Scottish free church minister, journalist and editor. In 1885 Nicoll was forced to retire from pastoral ministry through ill health, moving to London, where with the backing of Hodder & Stoughton publishers he founded the *British Weekly* with a view to engaging the free church constituency, which until then had been poorly served by journalists. "Hodder and Stoughton began publication on 5 November 1886 of the *British Weekly: A Journal of Social Progress*, a penny weekly with Nicoll as editor." The publication quickly accumulated a wide readership and Nicoll managed to secure a large number of influential scholars and writers. Matthew, "Nicoll, Sir William Robertson (1851–1923)," *ODNB*.

Sangster himself wrote in the *British Weekly* on three occasions: April 24, 1952, 6–7;

for his paper, and how he used to boast about the people that he had made. "I made him! I made him, through my paper!" And one day he wrote to Dr. Terman. He asked him to write in his paper, and Terman refused. And he wrote back again and said, "Terman, you must write in my paper. You must! I made Kipling. I made Barry. I could make you!" And Dr. Terman, that distinguished preacher, replied on a postcard, "Dear Nicoll, I always thought Almighty God made me and in any case I don't want to be Nicoll-plated!" Where do you want to make a name: on earth or in heaven? Or in heaven?

I went back to Scarborough a little while ago, a town where I ministered years ago.[29] And somebody in the congregation this evening mentioned Scarborough to me only an hour or two ago. When I go to Scarborough back to which is one of my old haunts, I paused outside a seedy little shop in a seedy little street. We call it in England a "fish and chip shop." You would call it a "seafood restaurant." But it was a very poor one, a very poor one. Let me tell you why I paused there. Seventy years ago a fisherman was drowned in the North Sea off Scarborough. He left a widow and four or five little children. His sister was working somewhere else. The offer of love had come to her. Life was opening out, full of promise. But then she heard her brother had been drowned and her sister-in-law was left with five children. She left the place where she was working. The opportunity of love passed her by forever. She went back to Scarborough. And those two women wept in each others' arms. People said, "You must put the children in an orphanage." They didn't want to do that. And then the other fisherman of the town, comrades of the dear drowned fellow, came to those two girls and said, "If you are going to try and keep the children why don't you open a fried fish shop? We'll help you. We'll let you have the fish, as we catch it, as cheap as ever we can. We will. We'll try to help you, for his sake." And so they did. And that lovely girl, that's what she was when she started; grew prematurely old in the searing heat of that fish shop. The children grew up. They didn't take much notice of her. She was only "Aunty," like a piece of the furniture. They didn't know the great sacrifice she'd made. The years went by and the children went out into the world. Their mother died. She was left alone. When I went to minister in Scarborough she was living in a little home, still penurious. There was a time of awful unemployment and the men seeking work, and making up the labour exchange,

September 19, 1957, 3; January 14, 1950, 4.

29. Sangster's ministry in Scarborough started in the summer of 1932. He left for Leeds Brunswick Methodist Church in the summer of 1936. Sangster's very first publications derived from his time in Scarborough, in the little-known newspaper *The Scarborough Evening News and Daily Post*. His first article, "Harvest Home," was published on October 1, 1932, 5. This type short article was reflective of devotional evangelistic style he followed for the next four years in that local newspaper.

used to queue up and used to line up past her little house. And she, out of her enormous pity and deep love of God, used to give them bread and cheese and cocoa in all that perishing cold. And one day one of the officials of my church came to me. He was a bank manager and she had a little bit of money in his bank. And he said, "Minister, you must go to Miss Webb. She is doing something foolish. She's only got £50 left in the world." $150. And he said, "It's running away. She's doing something! Go and see her!" I went, and I saw what she was doing: tackling those out-of-work men. And I said to her, "Don't do this. I beg you. Please don't. You will soon be in state of great need, won't you?" She said minister, "You want me to talk to God about it, don't you?" And I, who felt so sure that God was on my side, I said, "Oh yes, that'll do. You talk to God about it. I'll come tomorrow." When I went back the next day and I said, "Well, Miss Webb, it's all right, isn't it?" She said, "Yes, it's all right. I went to the Lord about it. I told him what you said and he said that I was to go on doing it." So I was beaten. So, her last £50 in all the world ran away in a river of cocoa. She never went to the poorhouse. That was her great dread. God worked miracles for that little saint and she would stay under her own roof until she died. And when she died there was no mention of her in the paper. No! No! No generous comments. Only the few knew the great sacrifice of her life and all that she had done. Only the few. No name made on earth. A name that I believe made forever in heaven.

Here is my final word to you. Here is my final word. Look, you grand young men and women, if you make a name on earth you really haven't made it at all. You'll be astonished how quickly people forget. If you make a name in heaven you've made it forever. If your name is written in the Lamb's Book of Life, if you follow your blessed Lord into the paths of loving service for others, if you seek to glorify him in all the ways that He will choose, however obscure your life is, you have made a name forever and ever.

I'm going to put a little test for you. You look to be an intelligent lot. I am constrained to put a test to you. I want to prove to you, if I can, how short the public memory is. I'm going to name to you now four names that were making headlines in your newspapers not long ago. And I'm just interested to know how many of you can identify who these people were that were making headlines in your newspapers not so long ago. And I would be astonished if anybody in this audience could name them all. Ready?

Stainthorpe, Stainthorpe.

Here's the second (I'll give you four): Dyer, D-Y-E-R.

Here's the third: Connielle.

Here's the fourth: Timrine.

No prize awarded, but tell me afterwards. You know why I'm pretty confident you won't know? Because it interested me during the day to ask a number of my friends here in the company—intelligent men, oh, highly intelligent—it is was interesting during the day to ask a number of my friends, you can ask anyway if you like, concentrated on the names by the people that know them, or think they do, well I just asked them, [me just being a visitor here][30], "Who was vice president of the United States when Mr. Hoover was president?" Two of them knew at once. The only problem was that they said three different things. And the other honest men said they hadn't even an idea.[31] Now, it's a very important office, is Vice President of the United States. Well, they're thinking so in San Francisco at present,[32] aren't they, and they were interested in Chicago a few days ago.[33] It is an enormously important office. It really is, to be the next man to the President of the United States. That's not a domestic matter; that matters in all the world. I'm saying that as an Englishman. But who they were—you've forgotten, you've forgotten. Oh, what is human fame? And when I see what people will do to get fame on this earth—how they will compromise with their conscience, how they'll do these shabby things and those shabby things—when I think of it! There's something as ephemeral as that. I am astonished.

I told you last evening that I ministered for a while in that grim northern city in England called Leeds.[34] And when I was in Leeds there was an argument going on all the time about a certain statue. We had a statue—we had several, but this particular statue was put up in memory to a man named Henry Richard Marsden.[35] He had been mayor of Leeds from 1872 to 1875. And when he died the people in 1875 were so proud of their mayor they raised £30,000 to put a statue up to him. Now, that doesn't impress you like it should, because they were Yorkshiremen. And a Yorkshireman, oh, he is tight with his money. This is a miracle. Oh, when a Yorkshireman opens his purse quite often a moth flies

30. Short inaudible aside.

31. Vice President Charles Curtis served from 1929–33. "Chronological List of Presidents, First Ladies, and Vice Presidents of the United States."

32. The 1956 Republican National Convention was held by the Republican Party in San Francisco, California during August 20–23, 1956.

33. Richard M. Nixon was vice president from 1953 to 1961 under the Eisenhower presidency. "Chronological List of Presidents, First Ladies, and Vice Presidents of the United States."

34. Sangster ministered in Leeds from the summer of 1936 to the late summer of 1939.

35. Sangster remembered his name incorrectly. The man he was referring to was Henry Rowland Marsden (1823–76), whose statue now stands on Woodhouse Moor, Leeds. Sangster first told the story in his sermon "Oranges Are More Precious than Diamonds," in *These Things Abide*, 23.

out! You see, it's so seldom. You ask any Englishman how tight they can be in Yorkshire. And these tight Yorkshiremen, they gave £30,000 to build a statue up. They must have thought a lot of him. In all the time I was in Leeds, in the 30s, they were trying to get rid of that statue. I mean it was in the way of the traffic. Nobody wanted it. People would write to the paper and say, "Move it to Headingly." That is one of the suburbs. Next night everybody from Headingly had written to the paper, "We don't want it." They said, "Move it to Chapel-town." That is where I lived. It was my turn to write. All the years I was living in Leeds we were playing draughts with a statue. When I was passing through in 1950 and I saw it was being moved at last, and I stopped the car and I said to a man, "Where are they moving it to after all?" And he said, "I don't know, sir. I think they are going to break it up." They didn't. They put it on a remote moor somewhere, where it will be the cream of the crop. And people that saw it removed had actually been present when it had been unveiled. Human fame, a name on earth. These people will sacrifice for human fame.

My friends, my young friends, do you want to make a name? Do you? You make a name in the service of your Lord. Do good work utterly for him. I beg you! And go forward and rejoice and follow him! And whether they notice you on earth or not it doesn't matter. The important thing is: your name is written in the Lamb's Book of Life. Anybody here that messed up their name? Anybody here inherited a good name and soiled it, anybody? The last word, that'll be for you. You can wash it clean, you know. You could. You could have a new name. You could. The Bible promises it. You could. If you're in that condition, tell God about these problems. Tell him. As this visiting preacher has reminded you that God himself has said, "To him that overcometh he will give a new name." Pray in his name.

Let us pray!

> Father, there are so many young people among us with
> all life before them.
>
> O guide them and help them, that they may make a
> worthy name,
>
> by thy power; a name with you forever,
>
> in the land filled with love.
>
> For thy name,

Amen.

CHAPTER 6

Guidance[1]

I WILL BEGIN WITH a word of apology this morning. I had no idea until the meeting was over that I had spoken for fifty-six minutes yesterday morning. It was my dear wife who told me; no doubt you guessed. She told me, I trust, with tenderness, but as is her custom, with great plainness as well. I mean, I wasn't in any doubt at the end what she meant. And so, I am beginning now with a word of apology to you; forgive me. The fact that none of you moved in that nearly an hour of my talking is only the latest illustration of your great kindness to us while we are here. I can only plead in self-defense that I had a very important and a very deep subject to press into one morning, and my heart was full of it. In time, so I trust, not sense, seemed all no more.

Anyhow, I stand before you this morning a penitent, and I trust, a converted man. And you will not complain, I am sure, today that I have kept you too long. You know our theme this morning, pursuing the quest that we're on: having the mind that was in Christ, being transformed by the renewal of our mind. We have come to this question of guidance. It relates in part to prayer, as we saw yesterday, and I asked your permission to defer it until this morning in order that I could give it unhurried attention.

How does God guide us? How may we make ourselves more sensitive to his guidance? We agreed together yesterday that prayer that left no part for listening must be incomplete prayer. We said that prayer in its essence was conversation and conversation is always two-way conversation; first one, and then the other. There are some people who come and say that they'd like to have a little conversation with you, but it isn't a conversation. It's a monologue; some addressing you as though you were a public meeting and at the end they

---

1. Sangster was a great believer in the active personal guidance of God in the lives of individuals. He first published on the subject in his 1934 book *God Does Guide Us*, followed by an article on examples of guidance in a popular British magazine: "Three True Stories of Divine Guidance," *Sunday Circle*, January 22, 1938, 85. Excerpts from this sermon were later printed under the title "How to Get Guidance," in *Secret of Radiant Life*, 248–55.

just leave. You haven't had a chance to get in a word edgeways. So, whatever it was, it wasn't conversation. Now prayer is conversation. It's speaking to God and its listening to God and hence its learning how to listen. If I had only ten minutes for prayer I would want to give six of them to God. Let us then think now together about guidance and the listening side of pray.

Some people, of course, don't believe in this at all. I mean, people who are not in our way of life. They don't think God guides individuals. Some of them who don't believe in that do believe in the existence of God, and what they might call his "general providence," but they don't believe in his particular providence.[2] They say, of course, "God guards the universe. He made it. He keeps the stars in their places. He holds together the vast frame of things." All that they believe. They don't believe that he's interested in your arthritis. They don't believe he's concerned about that dreadful road accident that has shadowed our minds as we've begun this morning. They don't think he's interested in that poor mother weeping beside her dear dead child. They seem to think that those are little things and that the great God of the universe can't be interested in that. We repudiate all that talk utterly. Nobody who really holds the Word of God would ever lend themselves to such thinking. God is great enough to look after his universe and take a father's care of his every child. There are some things we wish Jesus would have told us and he didn't, but he told us all that we need to know on that subject. He said, "The very hairs of your head are all numbered" [Matt 10:30]. So rest on that. We are not here this morning to discuss whether God guides. We know he does. We are here only to discuss how he guides. Well, God guides in six major ways, I suggest:

He guides through the Bible.

He guides through reason.

He guides through the church.

He guides through circumstances.

He guides through conscience.

And he guides through the inner voice or inner light.[3]

I need to look at each of those in turn. Sometimes what seems like guidance from one of them may leave us in some doubt, but when each of the ways of his guidance, or when several of them corroborate one another we need not fear. We can say within ourselves, "This clearly is our guided way."

Now I say first that God guides through the Bible. He has made his will plain for our race on all major issues in this holy book. I hope nobody will

---

2. Sangster wrote a little-known short pamphlet on providence in 1937, *Providence*.

3. These are essentially the same points as written in *God Does Guide Us*.

join issue with me when I say that we don't need guidance from an inner light or an inner voice over nine tenths of life because we've already received it in his Holy Word. Take the Ten Commandments by themselves alone.[4] What a large area of life the Ten Commandments cover. God's will isn't in doubt on anything that is plainly set down in the Ten Commandments. A great deal of the loose morality of the day would all be cleared away by simply respect for the Ten Commandments. A man who says he needs guidance because he's in some "jam," as he calls it, by reason of sexual looseness is not really in any need of guidance at all. He's either a conscious hypercritic or he's been so meddling about with his own conscience that it no longer moves with speed and certainty. I say again: a man doesn't need any guidance to keep his marriage vows; he only needs strength. Don't misuse the word "guidance." Remember, that in the Word of God, covering so many varied and important areas of life, God has given us his guidance. And when he gave those commandments, as I've said before, he didn't give them to a group of Semitic tribes and for them alone, but he gave them through that group of Semitic tribes to all people and for all time. To the Eskimo and the Negro, the German and the Jap, the Russian and the Jew, God has spoken. No amount of difficult circumstance or possible bias to sin ought to blind us to the fact that we have received authoritive meanings on all of those things.

We thank God for his guidance in the Bible. Yet I must say at once, because we must face the difficulties of this perplexing matter, it is perplexing in part that there are some questions on which the Bible does not give us as clear an answer as we would wish. You might say, "Ah, it gives the answer in principle, doesn't it?" And I am conceding the force of that point, except that I must add this: that on some subjects [it isn't as clear as we might wish.][5] Christian people might defer, they might. Christian people might honestly differ. The Word is there and the Word is sacred to them both, to them both. But the interpretation is different. And if you press me to give an example I will say that difficult gnawing question of our generation: whether or not a Christian man should ever bear arms, whether he should ever go to war. There are some with this holy book in their hands who say to me, "You know he can never go to war; a Christian man can't." And there are others just as seemingly conscientious who say, "Sometimes—they are rare times, but they do come—when a Christian man not only may, but he *must* resort to arms." And there you have an illustration of how two groups of people, similarly sincere, studying the Holy Word, could on this basis of interpretation walk a different way. We thank God for the Bible, for all his guidance that comes from that

4. Exod 20:2–17; Deut 5:7–21.
5. Unclear on the recording, but this sounds correct.

means we recognise how wide an area it covers. We agree that it still leaves some things to be decided by other means.

God guides, in the second place, through our reason. Never despise reason. Some religious people are prone to do, and I understand why they should feel that way because non-religious people have often abused their reason. What does the atheist do but to take the very reason which God gave him in an effort to disprove the existence of the one who gave it to him! Oh yes, reason, of course, can be abused. It is a precious gift of God. It makes us in some senses "higher than the beasts and but a little lower than the angels."[6] And coming from God, must ever be cherished. But our reasoning ought always to be with God. Charles Wesley, in one of his lovely hymns, uses this phrase: "Lay my reasonings at thy feet."[7] How clear it is. Oh reason, use that God-given gift, but lay your reasonings at his feet.

And I want to go on and say this: that in this mortal life reason cannot answer every difficulty. It can't even do it with a, with a praying man. It can't even do it with an apostle, and I can illustrate that in the lesson that I read. When you think of Paul, that he appears before us in this sixteenth chapter of Acts—and by the way let me say in parenthesis that this is one of the "we" passages; you notice as I read. Do you remember when we were talking about living the "we life" I said that there were "we" passages in the book of the Acts of the Apostles? And this is one of them. Luke had joined the party when this story was being set down. Now, Paul was a missionary statesman. There are some missionaries who are not missionary statesmen; they are real missionaries. They go to one spot of earth. They stay there maybe forty years. They gloriously do God's tasks in that area, and they are true missionaries. But they are not missionary statesmen. There are some missionaries who can do that work and glorious works of God on one spot of earth, but in addition they can carry the whole world in their mind. And if you were to say to me, "You must show me an instance of a missionary statesman of whom would that I think most rapidly, this week, in this place"—if it wasn't a Doctor Laubach.[8] There you have a great missionary who is a missionary statesman as well. Now Paul was the missionary statesman par excellence. He was seeking to get the gospel to cover the whole world as he knew it. He wasn't just out working the gospel in Corinth or in Philippi. He was thinking of the whole world. Can I sow the

6. Loose reference to Ps 8:5.

7. Last line of the second stanza of the hymn, "Lord, That I May Learn of Thee," in *CHPCM*, 446–47.

8. Dr. Frank C. Laubach (1884–1970), an American Congregationalist missionary of great repute, who was best known for his literacy programmes, especially his "Each One Teach One" principle, which is reputed to have taught 60–100 million people to read. See Roberts, *Champion of the Silent Billion*.

seeds of the gospel in this caravan? It's just setting out. It will carry the seeds of the gospel here, and there, and all the time he was planning ahead and thinking of the world. Now, he thought into Asia, the next place to go, right into Asia. "I'm ready." And then you notice how the Scripture says, Luke says, "We were forbidden of the Holy Ghost to preach the word in Asia" [Acts 16:6]. "Forbidden of the Holy Ghost to preach" is strange, but there it was. They were forbidden. So Paul said, "Well clearly, then, the next important places are the, southern shores of what we call the Black Sea." He says, "I think Bithynia is the place. Bithynia, it's an important centre. Oh yes, all that area. They need the gospel. Bithynia next. We're going to Bithynia. Ready?" And they are just about to set out to Bithynia when the Spirit suffered them not. "*No! No!* Not to Bithynia" [Acts 16:7]. Paul was beaten. All his reasoning, all the sense of the thing, every bit of foresight he had said, "Go there," and he was stopped, and stopped by God. Then he had a vision. In the vision he saw a man from Macedonia saying, "Come over and help us" [Acts 16:9]. See, that is the guidance. All his sense is there, but the vision said, "Come here." He listened.

Paul didn't know—and nobody alive could know at that time—that Bithynia and the whole of that area was to become a burnt up waste.[9] Nobody could have known at that time that the whole centre of the world was going to shift from Asia Minor to Europe, and the triumph of the gospel in Europe would mean the triumph of the gospel later in the wider world. Nobody could have known it. No man alive could have known it—not the profoundest man. God knew it. And there he was leading his servant even when his reason led him this way. "No, no, Paul! No!" And he [guided][10] him in what then was an unlikely way: to Macedonia. But when he went to Macedonia he went to Europe. And when he went to Europe, ultimately, it meant the gospel came to you.

9. It is uncertain to what Sangster is referring. If taken literally it could be a reference to the "great earthquake and fire of Nicomedia" (358 CE).

Ammianus Marcellinus (17.7.1–8), a fourth-century writer (English translation from Guidoboni et al., 1994):

"At the same time fearful earthquakes shattered numerous cities and mountains throughout Asia, Macedonia and Pontus with repeated shocks. Now pre-eminent among the instances of manifold disaster was the collapse of Nicomedia, [. . .] a terrific earthquake, utterly destroyed the city and its suburbs. And since most of the houses were carried down the slopes of the hills, they fell one upon another, while everything resounded with the vast roar of their destruction [. . .] And the greater part of the temples and private houses might have been saved, and of the population as well, had not a sudden onrush of flames, sweeping over them for five days and nights, burned up whatever could be consumed." http://penelope.uchicago.edu/Thayer/E/Roman/Texts/Ammian/17*.html.

For an interesting history of the Roman province, including the time of Paul and beyond, see Levick, "Pliny in Bithynia and What Followed."

10. Perhaps "steaded."

My friends, this is an illustration of how you need more than human reason if you are to understand the guidance of God. You will use it; you will respect it; you will not despise it; but you will recognise its limitations, and you will know that there are times when guidance carries you beyond any means that reason itself can reach.

God guides us in the third place through the church. There is stored up in the church an age-old wisdom. You all know very well that the church in some ages has been cold. And I know very well in some ages the church has been corrupt. And I am going to say this: that with all her faults the church is still God's chief instrument for getting his will done in this world, and you must be careful to ignore the age-old wisdom of the church. And I want to explain to you: why? Here is the fact of the matter. In the long history of the church there have been instances of people who have studied the Bible closely, who have reasoned on the Bible closely, who have been devoted and eager to do whatever they believe God's will was for them, but who, ignoring the counsel of the church, have said, "No! No! You can't do this," and all the sad things that have happened because of the neglect of the stored-up witness of the fellowship.

Last evening I was speaking to you about how people become saints, and I know some people who are accused of being cranks and don't deserve it. But while that is true, there are still people who are cranks, and one of the reasons why good people have become cranky and crotchety and eccentric is because they have ignored the stored-up wisdom of the church.

And if you, again, are of need of an illustration, I'll admit it: last evening the bishop in his kind word here mentioned the Anabaptists. And any of you that know [sketchily][11] the history of the Anabaptists[12] will know that sad time in the history of that sect and that country when the Anabaptists, studying the Word of God, came on the text, "Except ye become as little children ye cannot enter the kingdom of heaven" [Matt 18:3]. Now, bless them, they wanted to enter the kingdom of heaven, as we do. And they were earnest people. And they said, "Now, we must go by the Word! We must! We're going to stick to the Word!" And so they did. And believe me, in certain cantons in Switzerland—and I've been to the places; I know—men and women in their forties and fifties and sixties all gave up their work. The windmills didn't turn. There was no lady in the kitchen. They all went out into the streets and made mud pies as children and played "Ring of Roses" and did all those, to you and

---

11. Unclear.

12. Sangster is probably drawing from Bax, *Rise and Fall of the Anabaptists*. Anabaptism could be regarded as the first real fundamentalist movement within Christianity, following a heavy biblicist agenda.

me, quite stupid things.[13] And in the end the government of Switzerland, who had been tender toward religious convictions, and as they have nearly always been, in the end they had to intervene. They just had to. The thing was beyond all reason and we all say, my friends, "How did those good pious people go wrong?" They neglected the council of the church, the wider fellowship of the churches. Then: "You're mistaken. You are giving a literal interpretation to the words that Jesus never intended. He was speaking of the childlike spirit, the willingness to receive the wonder and the faith of little people. He didn't mean you to play with mud pies in your fifties. No! No!" That's how it happened. I know it sounds mad to us but that's history. And the church with her stored-up wisdom would say good things like that.

If you want it putting in quite practical terms today, let me put it this way. Suppose a young man, a young woman in your church and suddenly were to decide that they wanted to be a missionary, all on their own. "I'm going, I'm going to be a missionary." How important it is at such times that their sense of call be corroborated by the call of church. How important it is that they submit their judgement to the judgement of others, perhaps the circle in the church or in the Sunday school where they'd grown up. They come to their leader, that wise good man or woman, and say, "Mr. So and So, Mrs, So and So, I feel a constraint on my spirit to be a missionary. Do you think this is the call of God?" And so, in the fellowship, with tenderness, it could be talked over, their whys. And they will discuss it. You know that some people want to be a missionary not out of love for God; they just want to dodge the difficult routine they're in, like that girl I mentioned on Monday evening from the gas office. You know? She didn't like the dull routine of daily life so she thought, "I'm going to have a bit of glamour. I'm going to mission." Those calls need to be checked. Our motives need to be examined in the bright light of God. The living fellowship is able to do it. The church in her wisdom says, "You offer as a missionary. You say you are called of God. But there are certain texts the Bible says, 'Obedience is better than sacrifice' [1 Sam 15:22]. God works in amazing ways where your living now. Let's test it." The church is right. In that way mistaken calls can be prevented. So, though I'd say the church has been corrupt at times, let us bless God that God guides through his church.

God guides also by circumstances. We have never yet, even those who have taken years of thinking through this, been able fully to understand the

13 Bax, *Rise and Fall of the Anabaptists*, 58. This type of biblical literalism was behind the events described by Sangster in the canton from St. Gallen. Because the Gospels said that we must become as little children to enter the kingdom of God, some people adopted behavior like children, playing with toys and babbling like babies. For a comprehensive, modern history of the Anabaptist movements, see Snyder, *Anabaptist History and Theology*.

way in which God affects happenings. But that he does. Who among us can feel any doubt? Strange meetings occur. You come under the influence of a personality you hadn't expected to meet. Somebody makes a remark that just fits into your need. You look back afterwards and you say, "Oh, what a big decision turned on that seemingly fortuitous happening." Big doors swing on small hinges. You all know that. And God, again and again, has called his people into paths of service and guided them in the ways he would have them go, by circumstances, by meetings, by contacts that seem trivial at the time and yet afterwards seem so mighty in their effects.

And again, if you questioned me, who would suffice for an illustration? I think I'd take you for a moment to the University of Strasburg years ago, where they had a brilliant young professor. Everybody knew he was brilliant. Everybody knew. They said he could have any one of half a dozen careers. What would he do? What they didn't know was that there was a sense of unrest in the professor's heart. With all those, his conscience had been unquiet. But the voice inside him continually said, "You have received so much in your home, in your race, in your mind. What are you going to do with it?" And, though everybody else thought so successful a man would be so satisfied a man, he was the most dissatisfied man. Now God had also in that university a simple woman who used to tidy up the room. And she loved him very dearly, loved the Lord very dearly. And she used to read the magazine of the parish missionary society, a little green-covered magazine. And she didn't get just one copy for herself; she used to get half a dozen. She felt so sure that this was God's work that was being done. This simple woman that cleaned and tidied up, God used her! Think of it! And [he] guided her to put a copy of the little magazine on the professor's desk. Was it impetulant of her? When she emptied his wastepaper basket was it wrong of her to put just on the corner of his desk, that he might notice it, her little missionary magazine? And I think normally he went like that with it, into the wastepaper basket. But one day when the sense of disquiet was in him—"For all that I have been given, what am I going to do?"—he picked up the magazine and opened it and read of the enormous need of the people in Africa: the sleeping sickness, the awful tropical diseases, the this and the that. He read it and this is what he says himself: "It was all done in a moment! In a moment! In a moment, there was no long struggle." He said, "I knew at once what I had to do." He put the magazine down—listen—left his professor's desk, and re-entered his own university as a medical undergraduate. And he is now famous throughout all the world as Doctor Schweitzer. Something happened! Oh, what a big door to turn on a small hinge. What a seemingly trifling circumstance: a man picks up a magazine.[14] See how God works! Did the Divine hand guide that simple woman, putting the magazine down? Some of you doing the simple tasks of the church really don't know how important they are. You say sometimes, "That's all I do." "I just give out the magazine." "I just smile them in at the door." "I just sing in the choir." "I just . . ." Don't you know, and don't you know that if you do that with all your heart to the glory of God, his honor is involved? He says, "I'll make use of your service, I'll make use of your service." And when you get to heaven you will see what mighty use he has made of your faithful service, however overlooked it may have been.

God guides in conscience, in the Bible, by our reason, through the church, through circumstances. God guides in conscience too. Now the shortened common definition of conscience is to call it "the voice of God." But they wouldn't let you do that in any serious philosophical school today because they say that's too cheap, that definition, and it leaves many problems aside. It overlooks the fact that one person's conscience leads them to do one thing and one person's conscience leads them to do another. It can't just be called in that simple way "the voice of God." Now I remember one day a woman came to my door with a form in her hand. She said, "I don't want my child to be vaccinated. I don't believe in vaccination. But I cannot get exemption from my child's vaccination unless my signature is corroborated by a minister of God or a justice of peace. Will you please sign the form and say I am of clear mind and [lucidity]?"[15] And I questioned her, "You really do mean it? You are consciously objecting to vaccination?" She said, "I am." I could do nothing else. I'd come to sign her form. It was on her conscience. I had another visitor later that morning, another lady, who said, "I can't be with you now. I must hurry off. There is a little matter on my conscience: my child hasn't been vaccinated. It will be on my conscience if they missed her." See! You see how conscience, as we saw in the matter of law. There are conscientious objectors. There are conscientious volunteers. They are as conscientious as the other. There are men who have hated war with all their nature and yet as self, "I can do no other." I must stand in defense of freedom. And both of them have a right to be called conscientious. But they both are, and therefore you can't too rightly say conscience is "the voice of God."

14. Albert Schweitzer (1875–1965), a Noble Prize winner, was both a brilliant theologian, musician and author with eclectic interests, best known in theological circles for his *The Quest of the Historical Jesus* (1911). Originally he was rejected by the Society of the Evangelist Missions of Paris because of his Lutheran theology. He trained and became a medical doctor for the organisation, serving in modern-day Gabon. Sangster was probably referring to Magnus Ratter's account in *Albert Schweitzer: A Biography*. For an excellent modern account, see Brabazon, *Albert Schweitzer: A Biography*.

15. Unclear.

Nonetheless, my dear friends, conscience is a very, very precious gift of God. We would all of us go astray without it. It is constantly reminding us of the best things. It is that we have ever been taught—and, listen, I am going to say a bold thing, and I'll debate this with a philosopher anywhere even though it sounds absurd. I am going to say that even when our consciences have gotten muddled—and they have got muddled in many parts of the world—if a man's conscience is really consulted at the centre, right at the centre, you can still see the conscience as God made it. And I'll prove it this way. everybody knows in their own conscience, without being told, that kindness is better than cruelty. Everybody knows in their conscience, without being told, that truth is better than a lie. Where people hedge on those things is in the area of their extent. The most awful savage who's as unkind as he could be and cruel and wicked; he wouldn't be to his own tribesmen, to his own family. He knows he must be kind to them and truthful to them. It isn't that he doesn't know what conscience is; he only limits the range of it. And when Jesus gets into a conscience to educate it, he widens the range to the whole world. He says, "Everybody's your neighbour," and what we need to do is to see that the conscience is educated through the kindergarten to graduation. And when the conscience is educated, how clearly and definitely it guides us through paths of peace.

Those people who say you can prove anything through the Bible, those people who say that conscience can be twisted any way, those people who say we believers can talk ourselves into anything, they are false. They are demonstrably false. God is guiding us through the Bible, through reason, through the church, through circumstances, and through conscience, and the blessing that these means of guidance corroborate one another. They do! And only on that one major matter of conduct to which I have referred is any branch of the church, in any branch of the church, in serious difficulty to this day.

Now then, my dear friends, I come with my eyes, you'll observe, on the watch. You see I am looking at it. Now we come to what I call, as I began, the listening side of pray. How do you listen to God? How can you distinguish the uprush of your subconsciousness from the Word of God? How can you disentangle God's voice from the murmurs of self-will? Isaiah said, "You'll hear a voice behind you saying 'This is the way'" [Isa 30:21]. How do you hear that voice? How do you know it really isn't what you want—selfishness with a halo on? Well now let's look it because if we can be clear there, we can conclude.

My friends, we can ourselves sensitise ourselves to the touch and the voice of God. The more you read the Bible and get to know him there; the more you keep in the Christian fellowship; the more frequently you go to the Holy Table, as so many of us did the last evening and through the night; the more time you spend in prayer in his company, in thinking about him and talking to him; the more do you become sensitised to the touch of God, the more keen is your ear to the voice of God.

We are going to imagine the hardest problem that can arise in this matter of guidance. Here is a Christian man who really does want do to the will of God and he doesn't know what to do. Two paths stretch before him. Is it this one or is it that one? What shall he do? Well he will say, "Does the Bible give a ruling on a thing like this?" And the Bible doesn't. You know, it isn't one of those questions on which the Bible has given any. It isn't a question between right and wrong. The more you advance in the spiritual life, the less and less are you faced with questions between right and wrong, and the more you are faced with questions between the lower right and the higher right. When you've lived a disciplined life for years, you are not prone to some temptations. I don't say you're incapable of them; I stress the word "prone." You're not prone to some temptations. You don't want to run off with somebody else's wife. You are so happy with your own. You don't want to put your hand in another man's pocket, God forbid. His hard-earned money, you respect it as you respect your own. You wouldn't soil your soul with a lie. You know that leaves a mark upon you. Your not . . . I didn't say you weren't capable; I said you weren't prone!

No! The big questions that face us, as we advance in grace, is not a question between the right and the wrong. It's between the lower and the higher good. And when you are faced with a question between the lower and the higher good, the lower good is the wrong for you. It is. Now, here's a man facing it. And, because there is no moral issue involved, because one isn't right and the other wrong, you can't settle that by appealing to the Ten Commandments. The church doesn't legislate on a thing like this. They don't. You look at it in the light of your conscience, and even conscience leaves you uncertain. It doesn't seem to be a moral issue. And conscience deals with moral issues. And yet, you can't help feeling it might be wrong to go that way eventually. It might not be God's path for you. What are you to do?

Now, that's the hardest dilemma of the guided life. If I can be clear with you about it, you should feel that I have said all I at least can wishfully say on this subject. My friends, you settle that dilemma by what we call the "appeal to peace." And this is how you do it. This method was first devised among the Quaker people. God bless them, because they have always had a special concern over what they call "the Inner Light."[16] The Inner Light—and it is right for the

---

16. George Fox said, "Your teacher is within you, look not forth." Nickalls, ed., *Journal of George Fox*, 143. For a contemporary discussion of the Inner Light within Quakerism, see Ambler, "Light Within—Then and Now" (a talk to the Quaker Universalist Conference, Woodbrooke).

whole body of Christians to listen to them when they were talking about the Inner Light—now, here is the way we do it: get alone. You have talked it over with your friends and that hasn't settled it. You have studied the Word. You've consulted your conscience. The church doesn't rule on the matter. And yet, this big decision stands before you. It could. Get alone. Be quiet with God. Don't hurry, I beg you. It is a major decision that is going to affect the whole of your life. Don't be hurried. If it takes an hour for you really to feel the presence of God, what's that hour in a thing so important? Just wait before God. Just look at him and talk to him. Talk under your breath and say, "Father, I don't want anything but your will. Guide me. Guide me." And, if you just wait, you will find the discordant noises of the world die on your ear. And you will find the selfish impulses lose their power. And you will find that central ego which is pushing more and more to the side, less clamant, and "What do you want?" and "What will be nice for your wife and children?," that won't seem the chief thing. You will be concerned as to his will. There comes a moment—all of you that have any depth of spiritual life will understand this so easily—there comes a moment, when as, John Henry Newman said, "there are just two luminously self-evident beings, God and my soul, God and my soul."[17] Now, you are there. Now, look at him compounded of one desire to do his will. Now, follow this.

Now, using the imagination I told you about yesterday, the sanctified imagination, now, see yourself travelling this world and doing it. "This is the way I am going. I have made this decision. Here I go." See yourself! Come back. Come back in imagination and wait before God again. Now, in imagination, you are going the other way. "This is what I am doing. See! Here I go. I am doing that!" Come back again and wait before him. Now, apply the test of "the peace." Listen, if God has a will in that situation, if it isn't morally indifferent and he doesn't mind which you do, if he wants one not the other, listen, a deeper peace will rest on the path he wants. Is that clear? I didn't say "thrills." There might be pain on it! I didn't say "rapture." I didn't suggest he'd want a taker on the path. It might indeed be a hard world to walk. I said not "thrills." I said, "peace." On one of those paths a deeper peace will rest. Go by the peace. That is the way of God for you. If you were to say to me, having tried the test with all the care that we have suggested—if you were to say, "There was no difference between the peace," then I say to you, "The question is morally indifferent." Your Father is saying to you, "It's all right my

17. John Henry Newman (1801–90), English theologian and cardinal. Trained and served as an Anglican priest but became best known for his role in the formation of Tractarianism, his growing personal theological and spiritual development in a Catholic direction. Through much personal anguish Newman broke with the Church of England and became a Roman Catholic in 1845, eventually being honored with the title cardinal in 1879. A prolific theological writer. Ker, *John Henry Newman*.

dear, please yourself." It's not, it's not a major issue with God. But if it is—and I think it will be if you have been as concerned about it as that, I think it will be—on one of those paths a deeper peace will rest. Go by the peace. And, now my dear friends, in the space of forty minutes, I have told you all I can, in that amount of time. [Listen to it.]¹⁸

Let us pray.

Father, the minutes go so swiftly when we are talking
of these divine things.

But we are trusting, trusting thee to use this time
of fellowship together.

We do want to live the guided life.

We want to feel upon ourselves all the while the pressure
of thy guiding hand.

We want to know like our spiritual forbears, You.

We want to know that all we do is right.

We want that inward assurance that we are in thy will.

O Jesus, come into us more.

Mark this time of fellowship together.

Give us to know the experience, the wonder of this Indwelt Life.

Make Junaluska a name of golden memory to us all.

And send us out now on our guided way.

O guide us, O thou great Jehovah.

For our Saviour's sake.

Amen.

18. Unclear.

CHAPTER 7

He's Always the Same

He cannot deny himself. [2 Tim 2:13]

I WAS TALKING THE other afternoon with our mutual friend Dr. Billy Graham, and in the course of the conversation he mentioned a man we both know, though he knows him better than I do. And he said, "I place him among the five most spiritual men I've ever known. I like him very much. He's always the same." On my way home I fell to meditating on the phrase, "He's always the same." What did he mean? Did he mean that his friend's personality is always clothed in one garment; that he was always grey or always gay;[1] that there was no variety of mood in him? That would be very monotonous even in a good man. But he didn't mean that. He meant that his friend was not capricious, was not subject to whimsy, wasn't kind one day and unkind the next, with nothing to explain the difference. That there was a noble evenness of character about him; that principles that were valid for him on Saturday afternoon were still valid on Monday morning; that his personality was integrated and centred in the good. He said, "I like him. He's always the same."

My friends, it occurred to me that there is only one being, only one, within this universe of whom you could truly say, "He's always the same." The wisest man has gaps in his knowledge. The most kind is sometimes less than his best. Of God, the high and holy God, of God alone can you say, as Paul says here, "He's always the same" [2 Tim 2:13]. He cannot be other than he is. He cannot deny himself. He's always the same.

On that I want to dwell this morning to your spiritual help, as I hope. I want to prove to you that in the unchangeableness of God is the ground of all our confidence, the ground of all our progress, and the ground of all our hope. I plan to do it in this simple way: I want to prove it first by the rationality of

---

1. In the language of the 1950s and the context, the word would have meant "brightly coloured."

94

the universe, and then I want to prove it by the spirituality of God. First the rationality of the universe and then by the spirituality of our Father God. In both, I believe, we will discover his unchangeableness is the ground of all our security. Let me look at each of them in turn.

Let's think now of the rationality of the universe. If God were not always the same in the handling of his universe, life for us mortals would be impossible. If God were not unchangeable in his dealing with us in nature, science would be impossible. If fire burned today and didn't burn tomorrow; if water froze at this temperature today and at the same temperature tomorrow it boiled, science—life at the last—would be impossible for us. As the philosopher Hobbes said on one occasion, "If it wasn't impossible for us it would be short and brutish."[2] It is because God is always the same in dealing with us through his universe that we can build up a corpus of knowledge, that we can have science at all, that we can pass through the generations our gathered knowledge, and one generation can build upon the next, and we can advance in understanding of our universe, because it's always the same. If you ask it a precise question in precise circumstances you will get the precise answer. Some people say to me, "Ah, but of course an omnipotent God could do anything, couldn't he? He could have had another kind of universe than this."

My friends, not even God can do anything. It is shallow thinking that supposes that he can. He is held by his own nature. He is the most rational being in the universe. That's why it's classed as a minor tragedy that we've allowed the atheists and unbelievers to take that noble word "rationalists" and call themselves "the Rationalists." Oh, God himself is the supremely rational being, supremely so. Not even God—for he cannot contradict himself—could make an aged infant, or a square circle, or a one-sided sheet of paper. He's held by his rationality as he's held by his spirituality. He can't be other than he is. He's always the same. Now some simple people have said to me on occasion:

> When you preachers stress the firm laws with which God governs
> his universe, and when you tell us, as no doubt you have right to do,
> that God can't tinker with his universe in answer to some prayer

---

2. Thomas Hobbes (1588–1679), English philosopher famed for his book *Leviathan* (1651), written during the turbulent times of the English Civil War. Perhaps influenced by the bloodshed and strife, Hobbes tended to express pessimistic notions of humanity; all are fundamentally egotistical, driven by basic impulses like the fear of death and the desire for personal gain. Hobbes advanced the argument that in particularly harsh circumstances, where survival is at stake, it could actually be rational to kill before being killed. Life outside the structures of society would be "solitary, poor, nasty, brutish, and short." Hobbes, *Of Man, Being the First Part of Leviathan*, ch. 13, §9, line 9. Hobbes is deemed to be one of the founders of modern political philosophy and political science. Duncan, "Thomas Hobbes."

of ours, it distresses us. It seems to cut the nerve of our praying. There are times when we are in difficulties, and we want to pray and pour it all out to our Father, and then we think, "Um, but the laws of the universe will work on just the same. Your prayers can't alter that. The same thing will happen whatever you ask."

You say, "Preacher, you seem to cut the nerve of my praying when you speak of God as unchangeable in that sense." You sillies! You don't have the nerve of your prayer cut by being reminded of that deep truth; not if you've grasped it. God is still great enough to care for his universe and take a father's interest in his every child. If you believe that prayer changes things, you don't believe it more than I do, but I believe it in the context of this deep truth: that He's always the same. You think now. Let me put it in a picture, a couple of pictures. Every schoolboy—even the boys who are being so quiet this morning—every schoolboy knows that iron won't float. Of course he does. But if you go down to the edge of our beautiful Lake Junaluska and throw a piece of iron into the lake, it will sink. That is a law of the universe and it cannot be broken. Iron won't float. I crossed the Atlantic a week or two ago in the Queen Elizabeth,[3] that great floating palace of iron and steel. You know, you know, we have ships, great ships. They circle across the Atlantic like that. Iron won't float, but we have ships. How do we have ships? Have we broken the laws of the universe? Of course not. You can't break them. If you try to break them, they break you. All that man has done with his limited knowledge is to work one law in with another, and blending together those unbreakable laws, he can do things that to our forebears would have seemed like miracles. He can do them, respecting the laws of the universe as he must. Thinking God's thoughts after him, he works miracles. If men can do that with their limited knowledge and groping understanding, how much more God can do, whose laws they are, whose mind these laws express? In your dilemma, don't feel that your God is locked up in the universe he has made. Say, "He's my Father and he's Lord. I see the deep reasons why there must be unchanging laws in the universe. I see quite clearly that we couldn't live at all if it were not so." He isn't limited by them, and working one law with another, he works his sovereign and beneficent will.

3. At the time of this sermon RMS Queen Elizabeth, and her sister ship, RMS Queen Mary, now at Long Beach, California, was the largest passenger liner ever built and sailed regularly between Southampton and New York until the mid-1960s, serving as a troop ship during WWII. During her conversion into a university a serious fire damaged her beyond repair and she capsized in Hong Kong harbor and was later scrapped. Britton, RMS Elizabeth.

And if every schoolboy knows that iron won't float, every schoolboy knows also that iron won't hang in the air. You try that. You throw a bit of iron into the air and see if it stays there. "It can't," you say. "The law of gravity won't allow it. It'll pull it down." So true. But I've flown more than once over the wide Atlantic, and I've flown the still-wider Pacific as well. In a machine weighing many, many tons I've soared into the air like a bird, as you have done. And when we crossed that wide Pacific, that waste of water, how well I remember coming down in the dark, and the tiny coral island, a mere pin's head in that waste of ocean, an island I shall ever love because I saw flowing in that island, in the breeze, a Union Jack and the Stars and Stripes in mutual sovereignty because the island equally belongs to America and Britain too.[4] Down came the machine like a great bird, settled on that tiny island, refueled, took off again, going to Honolulu, to San Francisco, and brought me two years ago to you. Iron won't hang in the air, but we fly, we fly. Man, working one law with another, can do marvels our forebears would have said impossibilities. "Men will never fly." He flies. He flies. He breaks no law of the universe. He works one with another. I say again: if men can do that with their limited knowledge, how much more the great God whose laws they are? He is always the same in handling his universe. It must be so for our good, but still not locked up in his laws, still able to hear you when you cry in pity to him, still able to bend to you. And if it be for your highest good, to give you your heart's desire.

So much for the rationality of it. I turn now to the spirituality, the thing that concerns me most. Paul says in this letter, "If we are faithless" [2 Tim 2:13]. "If we are faithless." O Paul, up in heaven, "If we are faithless." We have been faithless! We know it! We know it! "If we are faithless, he abideth faithful: for he cannot deny himself" [2 Tim 2:13]. He's always the same.

My friends, every one of us knows how vacillating we have been at times, how we've wandered from the path that God marked out for us. Some of us who have been long in this way of life, trained in our Sunday schools, growing up in Christian homes, and yet, on occasion, we have wandered from that known path. God forgive us. We have been faithless but "he abideth faithful; for he cannot deny himself" [2 Tim 2:13]. Is that true?

Does he abide faithful? I must face a problem here in the same way that I had to face a problem when we looked at the rationality of the universe. I must face a problem: now we look at his spirituality. Is it true, honestly, that

---

4. Sangster seem here to be referring to the one-time status of Kanton Atoll (Canton) as a refueling point for trans-Pacific flights. Beswick, "Two-Ocean Passenger." Kanton Island Airport was still being used during the 1950s as a stopover for propeller aircraft. Following a dispute over sovereignty of the atoll immediately prior to WWII, Kanton Atoll and Enderbury were placed under joint British and American control. "Kanton Atoll." *Encyclopedia Britannica.*

he's always the same? Haven't all of you had experience, if you've lived any length of years at all, of tragedy in your life? Haven't you had dark hours? You see, is he always the same?

I was preaching a little while ago in the town of Newark, in England, after which you so kindly named your Newark in New Jersey. I was preaching in Newark, that old city, the other day, and when the afternoon service was over a lady came to see me ,spoke to me in the aisle ,with great sorrow in her face. She said to me, "Do you remember preaching in Whitby?" I said, "In Whitby? Yes, madam I do, but it was many years ago." She said, "It was the last happy day of my life." I said, "The last happy day of your life? Why?" She said:

> My husband was with me then. He was a good man, a local preach-er, a class reader. Our minister called him once "a great block of the salt of the earth."[5] He was a lovely man, was my husband; a working man. He took a day off from work to attend the circuit rally and we sat together in the afternoon. We were there for the great meeting at night. It was a lovely day. And we went home and the next morning he got up as usual and after breakfast he kissed me and he went out to work, and half an hour later he was carried in dead, killed in a motor accident. Carried in dead.

"Oh yes sir," she concluded, "I remember you preaching in Whitby. It was the last happy day of my life." And as I looked into her eyes I could read what was there. She was saying, "O God, he was your man. He was yours. Yours! He only lived for you. Couldn't you have taken better care of him? Couldn't you?" Had God forgotten to be gracious? In hours like that can you truly say, "He's always the same"?

Or, I was going through Bermondsey[6] the other day, and that's one of the poorer areas in London. I'd gone to share in the opening of a new church, and as I hurried through the slum districts of Bermondsey I thought on that great doctor of medicine who lived there until recently, Dr. Alfred Salter.[7] The name

---

5. Matt 5:13.

6. A district of London on the south of the Thames, near Tower Bridge, Southwark.

7. Alfred Salter (1873–1945), British doctor and politician, famed for his commitment to the poor of one of London's most deprived areas. Brought up in a strict Christian home, the faith of which he rejected while at university, though he maintained a lifelong stance against alcohol. An outstanding medical student taking numerous honors and prizes, his medical career seemed destined for international renown. However, in 1898 he moved to Bermondsey and came into close contact with the Methodist settlement's founder and leader, the Rev. John Scott Lidgett. Through the Christian witness of Lidgett and Ada Brown, who later became his wife, Salter was converted, joining the Peckham meeting of the Quakers. Salter established a general medical practice, working long hours amongst the poor and destitute. Salter was a strident pacifist and became a political activist and MP.

will be unknown to most of you but it is a great name in my country, Dr. Alfred Salter. Would you allow me to say, as a senator of the University of London for twelve years, that we still regard at the University of London Alfred Salter as the most remarkable man that passed through our medical schools. The gold medals and the fellowships dropped into his lap. All the specialists wanted him to specialise in their specialism—a brilliant student. When his course was over he wouldn't specialise in any of them. He said, "No, I'm going to specialise in the poor. I've been doing some of my practice down in Bermondsey among those poor people." Oh, this was the beginning of the century. This was long before welfare states were dreamed of. He said, "I'm going to live there. That's where I'm going to live." He was an atheist at the time; I'm obliged to tell you the truth. He did not believe in God. He was a militant atheist. And when he turned his face to Bermondsey it was inevitable that he should come face to face with that other great man in Bermondsey, that Methodist preacher Dr. John Scott Lidgett.[8] My ministerial brethren who are here will agree with me that purely intellectual conversions are rare, but they do happen, and this was one of them. When Salter and Lidgett came face to face, both of them dedicated to the poor of Bermondsey, two great men met, and clashed. One was doing it all for the love of Jesus and the other said, "I don't need religion to motivate me. I can do it for love of the people." And Lidgett said, "Salter, give me time and I will convince you. Come to my settlement one night a week.[9] I will argue with you if you wish. I will convince you." And when those two men came face to face, two great men met, and—listen—the man of God won! Ah, Salter, missed no opportunity in later life to say it. He said, "He mastered me. He mastered me." He did. By the sheer logic of mind Alfred Salter became a believer and still

---

A number of buildings and monuments are dedicated to his name in Bermondsey, e.g., Alfred Salter Primary School, Alfred Salter Bridge, and statues. Howell, "Salter, Alfred (1873–1945)," ODNB. Also see Brockway, Bermondsey Story.

8. John Scott Lidgett (1854–1953), British Methodist minister, known particularly for founding the Bermondsey settlement in 1892, having become aware of the gulf between rich and poor and the evils of poverty, poor housing and the curse of unemployment, while serving on the Wesleyan Methodist Cambridge Circuit. Lidgett was both president of the Wesleyan Methodist Conference in 1908 and president of the British Methodist Conference after Union in 1932. Lidgett received the Order of the Companions of Honour in 1933 in recognition of his outstanding contribution to Bermondsey. A road is named after him in Bermondsey. Turberfield, John Scott Lidgett, Archbishop of British Methodism?

9. Settlements were a distinctive aspect of Victorian England. Individual philanthropic Christians were encouraged to live and work among the poor and destitute, exemplifying the life of Christ by their actions, with the goal of alleviating poverty. Before the advent of the welfare state the settlement houses often provided daycare, education and healthcare with a view to improving the prospects of the poor in these areas. At a secondary level the houses hoped to provide opportunities to acquire knowledge and experience aspects of culture often denied to the poor. Scotland, Squires in the Slums.

stayed in Bermondsey for better reasons now. It was his wife who didn't like it. She said to him, "Alfred, do we have to live in the slums? Can't we live in the suburbs and you come up every day? Have we got to live here?" And he said, "Yes, of course. It's no good helping people at the end of a pole. We got to live with them and be their neighbours." She said, "Well that's all right, Alfred, for you and me but what about Joyce?" Joyce was their only child and a lovely little girl. And Alfred Salter said, "Well Joyce should live there too. The children of the poor have to live in these stinking slums. She must make friends with our neighbours too." So there he lived and Joyce, one day, caught scarlet fever and she got better. And she caught scarlet fever a second time and she got better. And she caught scarlet fever a third time—and she died. And it was a long time before the hurt look went out of Mrs. Salter's eyes, and it was a long time before we heard that great laugh of Alfred Salter. Oh, I used to think sometimes when I saw him—I didn't often see her—when I saw him, I sometimes caught in his eyes a hurt look which seemed to be saying to heaven, "O God, I was staying there for your children. Couldn't you have taken care of mine, my little girl? Couldn't you have done that, Father?"

Those are the dark moments of life, the really dark ones! Not the trifling little things that you sometimes call a "cross," and belittle the word "cross." These are the great sorrows of life: to you lose your mate, as the good woman from Whitby did, to have your only child snatched from you like that, to have your dearest certified insane. Oh, these, these are the dark experiences of life. This is what I want to ask you: Is he always the same, then? Has he not forgotten to be gracious? How do you handle yourself in an hour like that? When it seems as though your world is caving in, can you still trust him entirely? Will you, will you, even in the shadows, will you still trust him? Will you say, "No harm from him can come to me. I know from what [I've experienced of him],[10] He's always the same"?

This is the advice I give to you, my dear friends. I want to give you a little couplet, as it were. After my text, this is the best thing I have for you. As you know, no preacher has anything better than his text, but after my text this is the best thing I have for you. Take this away with you though you forget everything else: don't deduce God's character from odd happenings; interpret odd happenings in the light of God's character. Have it again: don't deduce God's character from odd happenings; interpret odd happenings in the light of God's character. Now this is what I mean.

To all of us, sooner or later, some dark experience in life comes and our weakness, our folly, our deep unfaith is to say at such times, "I was mistaken in

10. The recording is unclear here. This is what I believe he is saying and it is contextually appropriate.

all those years of the past. I thought I knew a good God, and this is what he's like." And we deduce God's character from that one strange happening. I say: don't deduce God's character from that one strange happening; interpret that strange happening in the light, in the light of God's character. Twenty, thirty, forty, fifty years he has blest thee. It has "been goodness and mercy all the way" [Ps 23:6]. This has happened. Maybe he didn't do it, but he allowed it. And he takes part responsibility even for what he allows, because it's his universe at the last. He's on the throne. He's allowed it and he wouldn't allow it if he couldn't bring good out of it. I, I will interpret this experience in my long knowledge of his faithfulness. He's always the same. He's always love. He can't be other than he is. And, he's still love, still love, even on this bitter path, darkly wise, but it's his path. All these waves have gone over me, but they're his waves, his waves, so I dive through them and emerge by his grace on the other side.

During this past week some of you, and some who have now left us, have been telling me of their personal problems. Not a few of you, not a few. I have discovered that many of you with smiling faces have a lacerated heart. God bless you for your courage. One of my brother ministers now gone home, down to the Mississippi area, said there, the other morning, on that very spot of the platform, he said, "I'm going. I did enjoy having lunch with you yesterday. There's just something I'd like to tell you." Oh yes, I'd had lunch with him the day before. What a centre of fun he was, not serious, full of exuberant gladness. He seemed like a man without a care in the world. And then he told me. He said, "We have a retarded child. She was born like it. There is no human hope that she will ever be normal." He poured out this story to me. He wept as he said it and my heart went out to him.

O my dear friends, I don't know you with the same intimacy but is there a dark experience in your life? Is there? Did your boy go to the war and not come home? Some dear ones of yours been killed or maimed in road accidents? We've been shadowed here this week by the sad news of friends involved in a road accident, only this week. Is there somebody you love in a mental hospital? Is there some big disappointment in your life, something you've longed for and it's never come, and it never will now? Has love passed you by? Are you born for motherhood and never held a bit of yourself in your arms? We all know our own secret hearts. This: have you been tested and do you find it hard to say, "He's always the same"?

Listen: he is always the same. That's what makes this truth so deep and rich and necessary. It's in that truth that our security rests. He can't be other than he is. He's infinite love. He's always the same, even in those dark experiences. He's always the same.

Some few years ago a strange thing happened in a home on Long Island. The home consisted of mother and father and a little girl aged fourteen. One morning when daddy was out at work the telephone bell rang. The little girl heard her mother answer the phone. "Yes," she said, "this is Mrs. Randolph March." Randolph March. Yes, that was the name. I haven't faked it. "Yes, this is Mrs. Randolph March speaking. Yes, that's the address. What?" She named an expensive furriers in 5th Avenue New York. "What? I'm to go there and choose a mink coat? Payment guaranteed by Mr. Randolph March. There must be some mistake. I've got a fur coat. My husband knows that. I've only had it three months." Then she hung up. And the little girl of fourteen saw her mother turn deathly white. And as she hurried out of the room she saw there were tears on mother's face. Now when her father came home that night—it was a Christian home—that little girl heard the nearest thing to a quarrel she'd ever heard in their home. Oh, she was put out of the room but she could hear angry voices coming through the door. She could hear her daddy saying, "Janice, don't be stupid, don't be stupid! So you think I'm involved with another woman? Where have I got money for a mink coat? I don't care what they say." At their evening meal there was a tense feeling. Something had gone out of the home. It never came back. You know, in a Christian home there's always a bubble, the gaiety that belongs to our Lord, a gladness at the heart of it. There were no quarrels in their home, but that girl said, "That gaiety never came back." And a few years later her father died. And when her father died, or soon after, the whole mystery was cleared up. Oddly enough there was another Mr. and Mrs. Randolph March living on Long Island, but forty miles away. It was clearly a mistake over an address.

And listen, listen, did that woman disbelieve her husband after fifteen years of married life they had together—happy married life, and years of courtship before that? Did she disbelieve over one telephone call? No! No! No! You see, she believed with 97 percent of her mind. She still believed. But in the other 3 percent there were termites of unfaith. Now and then it would come back to her and she'd harbor it, and it would breed, just in the 3 percent. And 3 percent is enough to take the bubble out of life, and all that glorious unshaken trust.

Listen to me, my dear friends. There are at least seven layers of our mind.[11] And you can believe in three, four, five, six. The sense of God—believe in seven—that's one of the things that's makes a saint: he believes utterly. He believes with every bit of him. He's standing on God. When tragedy happens

---

11. Sangster's understanding of psychology was primarily rooted in the work of Carl Jung.

to him he lifts his hand and says, "I declare this to be good unto me."[12] Those are advanced souls that speak that way. I'm not asking for that at this moment. I'm only telling you what the saints do. Of tragedy they will say, "I declare this as good unto me."[13] But I am saying this to you: it isn't enough for you to say to me, "I believe, Doctor. Yes, I believe in God." If you say that to me, I'll say to you, "How much do you believe? How much?" Five layers? Six? Six and a half? I want you to believe with every layer of your mind; to trust him utterly. Look at that cross. He loved as much as that. He stretched himself on the wood for you. He exposes in a moment of time what God is through all eternity. He loves like that. Can you doubt him, even when you think of the boy that didn't come home, the dear retarded child, the mental hospital, the denials of your life, looking across at an empty bed? Believe him. Trust him. He is worthy. He is worthy! He is always, always the same.

Let us pray.

O God, our Father,

on this lovely day and in this lovely place,

send us away asking ourselves,

"not if we believe, but how much, how much we believe?"

And if we find unbelief in even a corner of our mind,

help us to surrender it.

And err we leave this lovely place,

and come to utter faith in our unchanging God.

For thy name's sake.

Amen.

12. Probably an allusion to Dan 4:2.
13. Ibid.

CHAPTER 8

How to Make More Time

¹ And the child Samuel ministered unto the Lord before Eli. And the word of the Lord was precious in those days; there was no open vision. ² And it came to pass at that time, when Eli was laid down in his place, and his eyes began to wax dim, that he could not see; ³ And ere the lamp of God went out in the temple of the Lord, where the ark of God was, and Samuel was laid down to sleep; ⁴ That the Lord called Samuel: and he answered, Here am I. ⁵ And he ran unto Eli, and said, Here am I; for thou calledst me. And he said, I called not; lie down again. And he went and lay down. ⁶ And the Lord called yet again, Samuel. And Samuel arose and went to Eli, and said, Here am I; for thou didst call me. And he answered, I called not, my son; lie down again. ⁷ Now Samuel did not yet know the Lord, neither was the word of the Lord yet revealed unto him. ⁸ And the Lord called Samuel again the third time. And he arose and went to Eli, and said, Here am I; for thou didst call me. And Eli perceived that the Lord had called the child. ⁹ Therefore Eli said unto Samuel, Go, lie down: and it shall be, if he call thee, that thou shalt say, Speak, Lord; for thy servant heareth. So Samuel went and lay down in his place. ¹⁰ And the Lord came, and stood, and called as at other times, Samuel, Samuel. Then Samuel answered, Speak; for thy servant heareth. ¹¹ And the Lord said to Samuel, Behold, I will do a thing in Israel, at which both the ears of every one that heareth it shall tingle. ¹² In that day I will perform against Eli all things which I have spoken concerning his house: when I begin, I will also make an end. ¹³ For I have told him that I will judge his house for ever for the iniquity which he knoweth; because his sons made themselves vile, and he restrained them not. ¹⁴ And therefore I have sworn unto the house of Eli, that the iniquity of Eli's house shall not be purged with sacrifice nor offering forever.

¹⁵ And Samuel lay until the morning, and opened the doors of
the house of the Lord. And Samuel feared to shew Eli the vision.
¹⁶ Then Eli called Samuel, and said, Samuel, my son. And he an-
swered, Here am I. ¹⁷ And he said, What is the thing that the Lord
hath said unto thee? I pray thee hide it not from me: God do so
to thee, and more also, if thou hide anything from me of all the
things that he said unto thee. ¹⁸ And Samuel told him every whit,
and hid nothing from him. And Eli said, It is the Lord: let him do
what seemeth him good.

My dear friends, I come to my concluding thought in this series. Never, I think,
do I remember in my life racing so much against the clock. We have been all
the time trying to cover so great a theme in so short a time. You remember,
first of all, we must define the theme: the secret of the "Indwelt Life"; how to
have the mind of Christ. We wanted in fact to respond to Paul's admonition,
"Have this mind in you also that was in Christ Jesus" [Phil 2:5]. We first got
the subject on the way. Then we discussed how to begin clean and we saw the
sludge ship going down the river loaded with our sin, the outward grosser sins
and inward sins as well. We then studied how to covet, realising that to covet
the best things was one of the secrets of life. And then we talked on how to live
the "we life"; Jesus and ourselves together. Then we thought to make a prayer
pattern knowing the danger, there is in all of us, that prayer should become
selfish. So we thought to make a prayer pattern.[1] And we discussed also how
to use imagination in prayer. And then how to pray the affirmative way. And
then how to intercede: meeting God and taking a name at a time from our list
using them together as it were, in our warm believing hearts. And yesterday
we discussed how to get guidance from God: how to be sure what his will was
in our individual life and in our community.

1. No taped copy of this sermon is known to be in existence, therefore is missing from
this collection of transcripts made from rare recordings. The essence of this sermon would
have encompassed the four points mentioned and is probably represented by the following chapters of *The Secret of Radiant Life*: "How to Make a Prayer Pattern"; "How to Pray
the Affirmative Way"; "How to Use Imagination in Prayer"; and "How to Pray for Others."
Following the World Methodist Conference and returning to Britain, Sangster, as Secretary of Home Missions, challenged Methodism to devote itself to cooperate in prayer
and support the Prayer Life Movement. W. E. Sangster, "Fresh from the Home Front,"
Joyful News, November 29, 1956. Perhaps one of Sangster's most notable achievements,
especially considering the onset of his fatal illness, was the building and promotion of the
prayer cell movement, which only a year after its reinauguration on December 18, 1958
had two thousand cells in one hundred countries, with Sangster publishing a pamphlet
in support, *How to Form a Prayer Cell*. The quarterly publication of *The Prayer Cell Messenger* featured articles from Sangster from its first appearance in March 1959 until shortly
after his death in May 1960. These articles were gathered together after his death and
supplemented by Leslie Davison in Sangster and Davison, *Pattern of Prayer*.

Well, now my dear friends, I come still in a state of penitence, the state I described yesterday. But I come to you on this morning, the last of the series, conscious that I may seem to have over-faced you. You use that word in America; we use it in England. If you put more on a person's plate than they can eat, they say, "He's over-faced me." And now, I fear I may have over-faced you in racing through so many important aspects in so short a time. And indeed, some among you—some of my brother ministers in personal interviews—have not concealed from me that they wonder, in their busy lives, how they are to find the time for all this.

Well, I want to speak to that state of mind this morning: how you can get more time. People have suggested that England is very different than America if we have time for all this, then. And I want to say to you at once, "What's time for? What would you be doing with the time if you weren't using it to get the mind of Christ? What is time for? Why have you been given human life at all?" And then I'll go onto say, "It doesn't take all the time that some of you suppose."

When I spoke about the use of imagination in prayer I said, "Give one minute to this a day, one minute at the right moment, one minute for this a day." You know this doesn't take time. If you will see it, and build it as good habit into the same work of your life, till it becomes as much a part of you as washing your face in the morning and going to your breakfast, it doesn't devour unnecessary time. The only part of it that is time devouring is intercession, prayer for ours in service, doing things for others as God directs you. That takes time. But which among you would begrudge the time for that?

Nevertheless, recognising how you feel, I want to employ the time I have this morning in doing two things. First, to explain to you how you can get more time, more time. We all think that's over blown. This silly Englishmen is now going to make up a day with more than twenty-four hours in it. First, how to get more time, and then, secondly, how to use this more time that you are going to get.

You all know, I imagine, the name of the Rabindranath Tagore,[2] the great Indian teacher who put some of his teaching in parables. And in one of those parables he imagined himself a beggar. And he said this:

---

2. Rabindranath Tagore (1861–1941), Indian author, poet, artist, musician and Nobel Prize winner. In the late nineteenth and early twentieth centuries Tagore is said to have reshaped Bengali and Indian art forms with a version of modernism, producing paintings, sketches, literary works and over two thousand songs, and also founding Visva Bharati University in Santiniketan, West Bengal. In *The Religion of Man* (1931) Tagore defines art as "the response of man's creative soul to the call of the Real." According to his biographer, "The 'Real' for him always meant the real world of human feeling and experience, as well as a spiritual reality beyond but always running through that world." He was knighted in

I went a begging from door to door. And one day as I went the king came in his chariot, all splendent. O, I thought, this was the great day of my life. And the chariot stopped by me. And he stepped down and came towards me with a smile. And just as I got my bowl ready to ask him for something, he stretched out his right hand and said to me, "What has thou to give to me?" And I thought, what kingly jest is this, that he should ask from a beggar? But in my embarrassment, and that he's waiting, I took, I took, from my store one tiny little least grain of rice and put it in his palm. But, Oh imagine my pain at the end of the day when I turned out my bowl to discover one least little grain of gold.[3]

You see the meaning of the parable: whatever you give to God he'll turn it to gold. If your mean heart will only give him one grain, right: it's only one grain you've got. If you'll give a minute to God a day, he'll turn your minute to gold. But I say, "If you gave him an hour! If you give him an hour!" If the present pattern of your life doesn't allow you to do these things, to open yourself to receive the mind of Christ, you better remake your pattern. If you are too busy for this, you are too busy, too busy.

So then, let me first tell you how to get more time. First, prune your days. Of course, no mortal can put more than twenty-four hours in the day. Time is one of the great equalities. One man might live longer than another man but he can't have more hours in his day. Time is one of the great equalities: twenty-four hours in all our days. We can't extend the twenty-four hours but we can prune our days and many of us need to prune. What do I mean? Now you go over your day in the light of God. Speak with him intimately in your heart, telling him, "Father, I've got busy on the wrong things. I'm crowding out the things that matter most. I'm running here and there, when I should be quiet with thee. Go over my days with me and teach me how to prune my days."

So, cut out all your recreation. If God says, "No, son, I want you to use that time in recreation. Not more than you need, but I'm not asking you to cut out your recreation." But I notice that some of you—take one of these newspapers. Oh, the difference between an English and American newspaper. Some of your American newspapers, it's like carrying a port entry record. At the end of half an hour my dear wife said, "I'm going to take home, dear, one of these papers, to England." "Well," I said, "you going buy

---

1915 but later renounced it in 1919, following the British massacre of pilgrims at Jallianwahla Bagh. He denounced British rule in India and advocated full Indian independence. Tagore became renowned throughout much of the Western hemisphere, East Asia and particularly Japan, with his works being widely translated. Radice, "Tagore, Rabindranath (1861–1941)," *ODNB.*

3. Tagore, "Gitanjali Poem No. 50."

another case to take it then, you are!" All those papers they were selling in New York, it seemed, so many, there were.[4] I find that some of you sit over the paper, turning it over and over for an hour, and then you put it down and say, "There is nothing in the paper today!"

I notice that some of you are sitting and listening to the radio, not for anything in particular, not because you've noticed that something will be on for fifteen minutes at a certain time, but you are just sitting and listening to it, I suppose, in the hope that something good will turn up. What a use of time. And if it isn't radio it's TV. And again, it isn't a selected programme, "I want that. I believe there is something worth seeing." There, but again, "Let's sit in front of the screen. Perhaps if we sit there an hour we shall have a bright five minutes." How time is going.

O my dear friends, I speak to myself as well as to you. We need to prune our days. This precious commodity—time!—must be put to its best use. Remember this: no time is your own! Oh no, not if you are a Christian. If you're a Christian all your time is God's. It isn't, as a Christian, as though it's all your time and you say to God, "And I'll give an hour to you." Nothing of the sort! You've got it all round the wrong way. "You are not your own. You are bought with a price" [1 Cor 6:19–20]. All your time is his and he gives you time for recreation. So, get it right that way.

Somebody said to Charles Darwin's son one day,[5] "How did your father do the enormous amount of work that he did?" He was an invalid and yet he

---

4. Sangster was in New York just the week before on August 16 being filmed for a TV programme, answering questions posed to him on the philosophy of religion, recorded for Columbia Broadcasting. P. Sangster, *Doctor Sangster*, 265.

5. Charles Darwin (1809–82), English naturalist and geologist who gained notoriety for his then controversial theory of natural selection, and has gone done in history for his scientific demonstrations of evolutionary development within nature. His is work is principally accessed through his two highly influential books on natural selection and evolutionary theory: *Origin of Species* (1859) and *The Descent of Man* (1871). The latter work, while perhaps leading to less public outcry than *Origin of Species*, demonstrated clearly the implications of his theory for humankind, with his views becoming widely known, selling thousands of copies in the first year alone and occasioning numerous press responses, attacks, caricatures, cartoons and commentaries. A second edition was published only three years later. His ideas were not completely novel, building on ideas from the uniformitarianism of Charles Lyell's *Principles of Geology* (1830) and Linnaeus's theory of the fixation of species. His theory caused and still causes controversy among Christians with a strong biblicist point of view, as for many it seems to contradict biblical notions of creation. Darwin has been described as one of the most influential figures in human history. Desmond et al., "Darwin, Charles Robert (1809–1882)," *ODNB*.

An excellent contemporary overview of Darwin's legacy is a collection of essays entitled *Charles Darwin: A Celebration of His Life and Legacy*, eds. Bradley and Lamar.

Sangster was the first Methodist theologian to comprehensively engage with Darwin's theory with a view to recasting John Wesley's understanding of sanctification and

shifted mountains of work. How did he do it? And Charles Darwin's son said this: "My father knew the difference between ten minutes and a quarter of an hour."[6] Do you know the difference between ten minutes and a quarter of an hour? That first: to get more time, prune your days.

Here's the second thing: it's what I call my method of "planned neglect." This will make some of you businessmen shudder but you must hear it. I call it "planned neglect," and I heard it from a great lady violinist. She was a master of the instrument. Oh yes, she had studied at our Royal Academy and what a player she was. Somebody asked her once how she got that amazing dexterity with a violin and she said, "I did it by planned neglect." She said, "Oh, I'd get up in the morning and go down for breakfast. Then I would return to my untidy room and I'd first of all have to tidy the room up and dust this and that. There were a few letters to attend to, and this and that." And she said, "I did it all. And then the morning was gone but I had had no practice on my violin. And as the months went by and I was making such small progress on the thing I most wanted to do, I said, 'I'll put it first. I will come up and let the room be untidy and the letters for an hour or two be unanswered. I'm going to do my practice first.'" So, she did it by planned neglect. She caught up with the other thing later. She became a great violinist.

Is there anything more important than having the mind of Christ? That knowing him—maybe you will do a few less things than you did before if you follow this method of planned neglect, but the things you do do will be infinitely richer. It's only when we spend time alone with God that we have value for our fellow men. If you keep on going round and round, what have you got to say? "That's because"—and that's how your conversation becomes half empty—"those old girls saying the same things all over again." It's when we have time quiet with God we acquire qualities that make our company worth having. So, if planned neglect is the way to it, planned neglect. Have lesser things that you might have the more important.

Here's my third counsel to you on how to get more time. I want you to employ in a new way your unoccupied and half-occupied moments of the day. Now, however busy you are, I'm going to be bold and say that there are odd moments in the days of all of us, waiting for a train, waiting for a bus, waiting for this and that. In everybody's life there are moments in the day when you are just obliged to wait. You go into a restaurant to eat. The girl may be doing

---

perfection in the light of modern knowledge derived from the sciences. For Sangster such endeavours were meant as a way of maintaining intellectual credibility and relevance in the pulpit. For a full discussion of Sangster's reformulation of the doctrine of sin and perfection, see Cheatle, *W. E. Sangster – Herald of Holiness*, 92–169.

6. F. Darwin, ed., *Life and Letters of Charles Darwin*, preface.

her best to meet the needs of all the customers, but you've to wait. You've to wait, sometimes. Or, you're on the bus, you're on the train, you're travelling, and it isn't a long journey, maybe. It isn't worth getting down to a great deal of work but it is still useful time. It is uncovenanted time. Or, you are keeping an appointment and the person you're keeping the appointment with isn't quite through when you come. Those are all odd moments in everybody's day. These are what I call the "unoccupied moments." And these are what I called the "half-occupied moments." In everybody's day there are not only moments, hours, when our mind is not fully occupied. Some of you businessmen will be saying, "Oh, I should live my life like that. You don't know how fully occupied I am." I am still repeating it, sir: in everybody's life there are tasks that we've done so often that we do them semi-mechanically and they do not take up all our mind—the miner hewing the coal, the policeman walking his beat, the housewife doing the mechanical tasks of the kitchen and the home. Why, when I was in accountancy I could add up figures all day long—and had to do it sometimes all day long, and do it with speed, and do it with accuracy—and think of something else at the same time. And that isn't clever with me. Any accountant knows that it adds up, when you are used to it, in one half of your brain, and in the other half you could be doing something else. Even when you fellows are driving a car—and we are not now meaning in congested traffic, because then your whole mind must be on what you are doing—but when you are on a steady open road and cars going along you find your mind moving on to other things. I call them the half-occupied moments of the day.

I want to say this: that those unoccupied and half-occupied moments of the day are among the most dangerous periods of time in all our lives. And do you know why? Because, as any psychologist will tell you, it is just at that time in our day when strange fears rise in our subconsciousness[7]—when old worries awake, when nasty memories come back to us, when dreadful fears and negativisms store in us. The termites of negativism get into us in those unoccupied and half-occupied moments of the day. When your whole mind is on a task they're kept out, kept out by the preoccupation. But in the unoccupied and half-occupied moments they come in.

You know how it is when somebody's keeping you waiting for an appointment. You're seething. "They're keeping me waiting. The impertinence of it! Isn't my time as important as his time? And I'm going to be late all day because of this." And there you are fuming. And when the interview

7. For a discussion of Sangster's engagement with the subconscience, and its application to the doctrine of sin and holiness, see Cheatle, *W. E. Sangster – Herald of Holiness*, 105–30. Sangster discusses it in numerous places in his works, best represented however *Path to Perfection*, 72–76, 114–23, 139–40, 234–35.

comes up you're in no fit state to persuade him to by buy those goods. It's in those half-occupied and unoccupied moments that *fear* makes its way into you. "I've not been feeling well lately." "I want something to pep me up." "I thought I found a funny swelling here." "Eh, didn't I get up with a headache this morning?" You see what's happening? You see, your mind is never blank! Never! And if the mind isn't occupied, it's going to make room for what I call those "termites of negativism." They're waiting. And in they come! In some people, alas, they've so invaded that they become whiney and they're all the time say, "Things always go wrong for me. I think it will rain. It always does when I have a holiday." See?

Now my dear friends, for your health's sake—the health of your body and your mind—you ought to take heed of my words, that I am concerned, as you know now, with the health of your soul and with how we may, the more and the more, have the mind of Christ. And you've been saying to me, "We haven't time for all of this." And I say, "You have. You must have!" And I say, "You can have more time if you'll prune your days and those half-wasted occupations or cut them down to a minimum." And I say, "You can have more time if you will plan neglect: the neglect of less important things until the most important things have been dealt with." And I say this also: "If you will employ the unoccupied and half-occupied moments of the day, you will be astonished how much more time you will have."

And having, as I hope, proved that to you, may I have your patience, and tell you now how I would like you to use the time you now have? Now my friends, there are many methods of employing the time. I have described one of them in the current number of the *Readers Digest*.[8] I only admit that because a gentleman last evening brought up a copy of the current number of the *Readers Digest* and challenged me to own up to the article that was there. All I can say in self-defense is this, "That while it's a great honor to be in the *Readers Digest* again, they've not only digested the article, they've predigested it as well." And I honestly wonder whether the most honest reader will get out the method I was trying to teach. The method, if you would allow me, I would like to teach to you now. You see here that we are going to get more time and we are going to use those uncovenanted moments, those moments that come unexpectedly when you're in—you men spend so much time in your cars—when you're in a traffic jam. You know, when you look ahead and think, "Oh, half a mile of us, how many times will that light have to turn red and green before I get over?" And there you are fuming away. Be calm, brother. You won't get over any quicker fuming like that. You're doing yourself harm. In moments like that how you are going to employ your time?

8. W. E. Sangster, "Treasurers of Meditation," *Readers Digest*, September 1956, 109–10.

Now one of my systems is to use key words. I'll tell you how I first did it but you can do it your own way. And, being so intimate with you, I took the aspects of the mind of our Lord that we've been discussing as they're set down. You need to see to Galatians: love, joy, peace, patience, kindness, goodness, faithfulness, humility, self-control [Gal 5:22–23]. Nine of them, and I reduced them to seven, if you will forgive me, because there are seven days in the week and I wanted a key word for every day. But some of the words I had to change because I wanted to put them into alphabetical order. It's easy to remember things when they're in alphabetical order: a, b, c, d, e, f, g. Begin on Sunday, end on Saturday. So I called love "affection," and I made out a list like this: affection, benevolence, calmness, discipline, endurance, faithfulness, gratitude. They're all aspects of the mind of Christ, all of them. And so, whenever I have those unoccupied or half-occupied moments—when I'm held up in that traffic jam, when somebody keeps me waiting—instead of fuming and thinking how important I am to be kept waiting.

O my dear friends, I've almost got to the point when I can almost enjoy being kept waiting. And I say to myself, "What's today?" Right away, leaving no time for those germs of negativism to get in, I say at once to myself:

> What's today? Saturday? G—gratitude! Oh, gratitude! What a lot I have to be grateful for: for my health, for my good wife, for children that love the Saviour, for children who have married others who love the Saviour, for being at Junaluska, for seeing my dear American friends again. Oh, I don't mind how long he keeps me waiting. I'll never get to the end of this. There's so much to be grateful for.

Turn it over in your mind. Turn it over. Glow with gratitude. See how good it is to be alive. Think of the mercy of God streaming on you even when you're in trouble. It is true, Bill. Bill's come back and he's sitting here.[9] Even when you're in trouble there are things to be grateful for. Dwell on them.

Or, maybe the day is Wednesday and I think:

> Discipline. Oh, I do admire self-control; the power of Jesus in you to say "No" to passion. You can't be exempt from temptation. And you must never confuse temptation with sin, though some people do. But to say "No" to it; never to finger it, never to gloss your imagination in it, never to toy with it; the moment you recognise it, to blast it with a prayer. Oh, the disciplined life. When you're pulled upon, as Jesus was so often by people needing his

---

9. It has not been possible from the little information given to provide information about the person referred to.

help, from one and another of them, to remain calm in him, to give your whole mind to each one in turn, to remain disciplined, how good it is.

So you see, my dear friends, you, if you cared to use this method, could employ those unoccupied and half-occupied moments to draw the light of Christ into you. And listen: you'll build a barrier against many evil things and among other things against nervous breakdown. Everybody who has had a nervous breakdown, and anybody who has lived with someone that has had a nervous breakdown, knows how occupied a nervous person is with themselves. No thought goes out to stay out. It always comes back, like a type of mental cannibalism, to feed on themselves. You know why that is? This is the sickness begotten of self-centredness.[10] But when you are thinking to have the mind of Christ you have built great barriers against that kind of thing. Health comes in and wholeness with Jesus. Oh yes. You, at least, will not be sick of psychosomatic sickness. You have a barrier against that, and all those evil germs that could get into your mind and create those many nervous diseases that there are, and get in in those unoccupied and half-occupied moments when you are feeling this lump, and wondering about this. All those moments are now employed to receive the mind of Christ.

In the World Methodist Building, this new and lovely building that you have all visited, I suppose, or will visit, you will see, if you go, a bust of my friend the distinguished artist Frank Salisbury.[11] And Frank Salisbury has on the walls of his own home in London a glorious picture of a bishop. I never go to see him but I linger by that painting of Bishop Brindle.[12] That's

10. While most present-day psychiatrists and psychologists would probable see nervous breakdown as a part of a wider picture of a temporary depressive illness and would therefore probably take exception to Sangster's views, a recent controversial and influential book challenges the tendency to ascribe the term "depression" to what was in Sangster's day called a "nervous breakdown." See Shorter, *How Everyone Became Depressed.*

11. Francis Owen Salisbury (1874–1962), a distinguished English artist and devoted Methodist. One of his most famous works, *Henry VIII and Catherine of Aragon before Papal Legates at Blackfriars, 1529*, was placed prominently in the House of Lords. Salisbury is credited with being a master of depicting large crowds. However, he had a most notable career as a portrait painter depicting distinguished clientele at home and in the US, including five presidents of the United States, five British prime ministers, and three archbishops of Canterbury. He painted Winston Churchill more frequently than any other artist. At the request of President Obama the portrait of President Harry S. Truman was hung in the White House Cabinet Room in 2009, normally housed at the Harry S. Truman Museum and Library, Independence, Missouri. Frank Salisbury exhibited at the Royal Academy seventy times. Bunting, "Britain's Painter Laureate." Also see Noble, "Salisbury, Francis Owen (1874–1962)," *ODNB.*

12. Bishop Robert Brindle (1837–1916), English Roman Catholic army chaplain, priest and bishop. An excerpt from the speeches from his funeral, which was a full military

his name. Oh, what a holy face! And Frank Salisbury told me the story about it. There was a mistake one day over the appointment, over the sitting. The bishop, an exceedingly busy man—exceedingly busy with all his diocese to care for, the care for all the churches pressing on him—came at the time he understood. It was a mistake. He had to wait four hours, four hours. Frank Salisbury tells me that when he went in he didn't know how to look at him, for keeping so busy a man waiting four hours. He had come all the way from Nottingham but he said:

> When I went into the room all my apologies seemed to die on my lips. His face, always was so holy and rusted, seemed more holy and rusted than ever. I could see heaven shining in it and when I began my apology he brushed them all aside and said, "Oh, I'm busy of course but, my dear brother—speaking as one Christian to another, you won't misunderstand me—I'm always grateful when unexpected moments come in which I might commune with my Lord. Did you say four hours? It doesn't feel like that to me. Oh, I have had a wonderful time. You're ready? I'm ready too."

This is what Frank Salisbury said to me: "I painted two. I did. I painted one for the diocese which had commissioned it, and then I painted one for myself, so that I could look at that holy face and be reminded of the secret of his love."

That's the way to it, really. That is the secret to the radiant life. It is only one of the many gains of this kind of living. Wouldn't it be wonderful, my dear friend, for you in your stressful life, if it is that, instead of fuming and worrying, you also could receive the inward peace and then "the earthly part of you," as our hymn says, "The earthy part of you would glow with the fire divine."[13]

Now I want to say, "If you had this quality of life you can't help perfecting other people." All your service will be enriched, even if you do less, and I'm admitting that you may do less. Yes, if you follow this way you may do less, a little less. What you do will be infinitely richer because if Christ is in you then one word from you will be potent. And one smile will be mighty because the

---

funeral, a rarity for a bishop, further illustrates the bishop's pious character: "What has struck me most in Bishop Brindle is his childlike piety and intense faith. He has always kept a child's heart in his dealings with Almighty God. His duty to God always took the first place. Open-hearted, open-handed, simple and straightforward, it is no wonder that he aroused in all, from the highest to the lowest, an ardent admiration and a loyal and devoted friendship. Spotless in mind and heart, and never hesitating a moment in doing the right thing, he had a Christ-like charity, and a father's heart towards the weak and failing. A great sympathy went out from him for anyone in distress." "The Late Bishop Brindle, D.S.O. A Military Funeral," *The Tablet*, July 8, 1916, 11.

13. Final lines of the third stanza of the hymn "Breathe on Me Breath of God," by Edwin Hatch (1835–89).

light of Christ is so potent that when it's there it works. You won't have to look around wondering who I can do a bit of good to. You know, people that get up in the morning wondering who they could do a bit of good to are people I dispose to Dodge, really. But if our Lord is dwelling in you, without even thinking about doing good to people you'll do them good just by going about. They sit on the same bus as you. You just pass your bag to the porter, you just buy some goods over the counter. Something travels! It does! If this is the light of God, it can travel on a word, it can travel on a smile, it can travel on a look. It is so potent because it is the light of God. I do not often feel encouraged in my own spiritual life. I'm conscious, as most of you are, I suppose, how far there is to go. But I can recall one or two little incidents in my life, trifling silly things—you'll say afterwards, "What did he want to tell us that for?"—but which have been of encouragement to me. And I recall one occasion when our maid came up to my study and said, "The milkman wants you." And I said, "The milkman wants me. No, Kathleen, you've misunderstood him. It's Mrs. Sangster he wants. The milkman wouldn't want me." She said, "He said you." So, I said, "Dear, I think you are wrong. I don't know the man. I've only taken the milk in once or twice when I've chanced to be at the door and he came. But of course I'll come." The moment I got to the door and saw the milkman I knew he was in trouble. He had no milk but a terrible look on his face, and I went up to him and put my arms on his shoulders and I said, "You're in trouble." And he said, "O sir, my wife! We went to bed last night as happy as anything and she as well, and I woke up this morning and she was dead at my side. O sir, I have nowhere to go, but I wanted to come and see you." And afterwards, long afterwards, when I thought on it—I think I've only taken the milk in once or twice, but he must have known I loved him, that I had a real affection for him, and in a moment of great need he turned to somebody he was inwardly sure loved him. People will do that.

Is this our Lord, stays to dwell in us, stoops lower than when he stooped to the manger, comes into our soiled hearts. When Jesus does that it isn't you anymore. No, it's your former personality, but He's in you, and I say, a smile and a word; your demeanor speaks of him. Emerson[14] might say to you as he said to one other, "It isn't your words that matter to me. What you are speaks to loud in my ears."[15] And what could speak louder than the life of God in the soul of man?

14. Ralph Waldo Emerson (1803–82), American New England philosopher, poet and essayist responsible for the central ideas of the transcendentalist movement. He published his key thoughts in *Nature* in 1836, though he is perhaps most famous for his 1855 poem "Song of Myself," which remains among the most admired and influential poems in American literature. Holmes, *Ralph Waldo Emerson*.

15. The original quote is most likely to be, "What you are stands over you the while,

So I conclude, my dear friends, and pray God that within these hurried, discursive at times, almost breathless expositions of something, in which my heart is full, that God in his mercy will bring blessing to your soul.

Let us pray.

O God, our Father,

So, all our time is thine.

Help us to use it for thee.

Help us to prune our days, have things in their right priority.

Employ those unoccupied and half-occupied moments for thee.

And, so, by the lure of strong desire may we draw in the life of God

and pass it out in blessing to many others.

For thy name's sake.

Amen.

---

and thunders so that I cannot hear what you say to the contrary." "Social Aims," in *The Complete Works of Ralph Waldo Emerson,* http://www.rwe.org/social-aims/.

CHAPTER 9

The Church[1]

THE FIRST LETTER OF Paul to the Corinthians in chapter 11 at verse 22: "Despise ye the church of God?"

I have often noticed both in England and America when I have been passing through the smaller towns and the big cities as well, that when you come to a big intersection of the streets you often notice, on the four important corners, a bar on this corner, a movie theater on this corner, a big store on this corner, and a church on that. A bar, and a movie theater, and a store, and a church. Everybody knows what the bar is for. Everybody knows what the movie theater is for. Everybody knows what the store is for. But what is the church for? What is it for?

There are people in both our nations that have no use for the church of God at all. There are men who say sometimes in public that it wouldn't be any loss to the nation if all the churches and Sunday schools were closed overnight. There are people that can see no purpose whatever in the church of God.

My friends, I would like to ask you this question this evening: Suppose tomorrow when your vacations are over and you are back home again, suppose you were to fall in with one of those people. Suppose they were to say to you in honest simplicity, "What is the church for?" What would you say? You couldn't go into deep theology because they don't understand it. You couldn't go deep into the Word of God because that is a strange book to them. You must keep within the orbit of their own ideas. You must speak to the level of their intelligence. What would you say to them in answer to the question, "What is the church for?"

---

1. A version of this sermon was preached by Sangster shortly after his return from Junaluska. The occasion was the opening of Upwell Methodist Church, near Wisbech, Cambridgeshire, England on September 25, 1956. A recording of that sermon is in the possession of the author. A comparison of the two sermons will give vital information to students of homiletics of how Sangster adapted and delivered the same sermon to two vastly different groups of hearers.

Let me give you some indication of the way in which I would answer it. I think—keeping to their ideas, knowing that I couldn't tell of the things that are most precious to me—I think I should begin by saying, "It makes sense of life. It makes sense of life." You see, everybody over forty, and lots of intelligent people before they're forty, realise that the big gnawing questions of life, the questions that have tormented the minds of man ever since he began to think, are not such questions as: "Who shall I marry?"; "What shall I work at?"; "Where shall I live?" Important as those questions are in their way, but the big the gnawing questions that matter at the mind of man are questions like these: "Who am I?"; "Why am I here?"; "What is life for?"; "What comes after this?" I say again, every man over forty and many men before they're forty, intelligent they be, know that these are the deep, the hard, the basic questions of life and, somehow or other, you must have them answered. They'll try the other three corners of the street and see.

Go in bar and ask them, "What is life for?" Now picture you're the man. They'll discuss it with you, some of them a whole evening, over a glass of drink. And you'll come out as you went in, no further on. They don't know what life is for.

Go in the movie theater, have a chat with that nice lady who sits in a glass case just inside the door. Say to her through the little pigeon hole, "Miss, I have come here this evening to discover the meaning of life. Can you tell me the meaning of life?" And she will think you are mad also, and she'll lean forward and say, "Look here, we are not here to explain the meaning of life; we are here to help you to forget the beastly thing for a couple of hours."

Go into the store and ask them. You know, in these big stores they have young ladies sitting in a desk. "Information," it says over them. I was in a store in New York recently, where it not only said, "Information," it said, "Ask me anything."[2] Well, that's fair enough isn't it? Go up and ask her. Put your elbow on the counter and say, "Excuse me, Miss, what is the meaning of life?" And she'll call the porter and have you put out. Oh no! They don't know the answers—not in the bar, not in the movie theater, and no, no, not in the store.

They know! They know in the church of God. This is what I would say to anybody that sees no use for the church of God and wonders what we are here for: "We are here, we are here first, to make sense of life. In the church, and nowhere else as far as I know, will they know how to make sense of life. We'll tell you who you are, and why you are here, and where you're going. We know the answers not because we were clever to discover them ourselves, but because God in his infinite mercy has given us his Eternal Word, and given

---

2. This is a clear indication that the sermon was preached after his visit to Columbia Broadcasting, New York, on August 19, 1956.

us his fellowship. He bent to our necessities and in him we know the answers to the deep questions.

I was preaching in Frankfurt some time ago, Frankfurt am Main in Germany, preaching in one of our great Methodist churches there. On my way to the appointment I went across the big park in Frankfurt. They call it the "Tiergarten."[3] And, as I hurried across the park, I suddenly remembered it was here that that historic conversation took place. Here, in this very park. I had forgotten Schopenhauer, the distinguished German philosopher, used to live in Frankfurt.[4] He was a pessimist. He saw everything grey. He could never bottom the mystery and meaning of life. He wondered if it had any. Incidentally, he hated women.[5] He wouldn't have had them near him. He'd be uncomfortable where I am tonight. He wouldn't have them near him and he had that "sudden appearance" that all men have on his clothes and person where there isn't that hand of a good women somewhere. So, putting it mildly, the truth is, he looked like a tramp. And he used to sit on a bench in that park in Frankfurt meditating on the problems of life. And the park keepers used to notice this old tramp and wonder who he was. And one day one of them, in the midst of his reverie, put a hand on his shoulder and said, "Who are you?" And Schopenhauer awoke out of the reverie and said with awful earnestness, "Who am I? I wish to God I knew."[6]

"Who am I? I wish to God I knew." That's the question that is unspoken in the minds of multitudes. Those who are not in this way of life, those who do not know Jesus, those who are not glad to frequent his church, they don't know who they are, and why they are here, and where they are going. And they can't, they can't make sense of life. What a ministry we have. Oh, isn't it wonderful to think that for anybody who will come in our Lord's name we can make sense of life. We can tell them that there are two ways stretching

---

3. Now called "Zoo Frankfurt."

4. Arthur Schopenhauer (1788–1860), best known for his work *The World as Will and Representation* (1818). In his retirement years Schopenhauer moved to Frankfurt and lived a life of strict routine, often found in outdated clothing, totally captured by his studies, most particularly towards the end of his life the natural sciences. See Lewis, *Arthur Schopenhauer*, 160.

5. Sangster was probably referring to Schopenhauer's *On Women* (1851). See also Thomas Grimwood's essay on Schopenhauer and women, "Limits of Misogyny."

6. Though this quote is cited by numerous other authors, often in sermons, but none earlier than Sangster, none provide a reference. Sangster was probably reliant on be William Wallace's biography of Schopenhauer, *Life of Arthur Schopenhauer* (1890), written only thirty years before Sangster engaged so enthusiastically with philosophy during his BA studies, and around forty-seven years before he took his MA in philosophy. This was the standard English text within the UK until the late twentieth century. Lewis, *Arthur Schopenhauer*, 11–12.

before us: a way that leads downwards to the beasts, and the way that climbs upwards to the heights. You can tell them that no man can find that upward path by himself but that Jesus our Saviour will come in response to a man's appeals.[7] He will take his hand and lead him up and on. You can tell them that all of us are morally accountable at the last, that someday we must come to the last audit, that we can have Jesus now as our Saviour or someday we must have him as our judge.[8] You can tell them who they are, and why they're here, and what comes after this.

In the headquarters of the British and Foreign Bible Society in London—a building I know so well; I am the vice president of the society—in that building there, they have the most precious collection of Bibles, about as doubtless you have at the headquarters of the famous American Bible Society. We have in London a Testament that is opened regularly, a Testament which no one can read, no one can read it.[9] It was made many years ago by one of our Methodist missionaries who went out from England to a tribe of Red Indians in Canada, became their friend, became their father in God, learned their strange language, reduced it to writing, translated the New Testament. Generations ago the Bible Society was so proud to take it. And that tribe of Red Indians had the Word of God in their own tongue. But everybody who spoke that tongue has long since died. Nobody speaks it now. It's a mystery language. The Testament is there. It's full of truth and no one can read it.

My friends, to watch the people passing those busy intersections of streets, in our smaller towns and in our big cities, they see the four corners of the street: the bar, and the movie theater and the store and the church. They understand three corners of the street, but that other corner, it's a riddle. It contains the Word of Life. There is the message they need but it is a mystery to them. Our task: to draw them in, to say, "Come to this corner. Here we have counsel for you. Here and only here, you can make sense of life."

Here's the second thing I say. Not only do we claim in the church of God to make sense of life; we claim this also: that we, in God's name, give joy to life. It would strike them as strange, I am sure, to these people that have no use for us. Joy? If you were to invite them to a night out, well, according to

---

7. An echo here of Sangster's anthropology, a revision of John Wesley's synergism. See Cheatle, *W. E. Sangster – Herald of Holiness*, 105–30 (119–30).

8. Sangster's concept of the afterlife was quite controversial within the branch of Methodism that subscribed to an emphasis on Christian perfection. This was one of the key points of conflict with the Holiness Movement. See Cheatle, *W. E. Sangster – Herald of Holiness*, 80–83. He also clarified his position just one year after Junaluska in a short little-known article, "The Probation of Life," in *The Great Mystery of the Afterlife*, 99–105.

9. The archives remained at the society's London headquarters until 1985 when the library and archives were transferred to Cambridge University Library on permanent loan.

their view they might think of the bar; they might think of the movie theater, that you could see a good wholesome film and wanted to take them to see it; they might think that you were going to buy something for them in the store. But a night out, if you want to take them to church, it would seem to many of them to be a bad joke.

Let me tell you this, quite definitely, with a sober mind, with no exaggeration whatever: the secret of joy, this hidden and wonderful spring, is in our gospel, it's in the church, and it's there and nowhere else. After this morning's address a lady, herself a teacher of English in one of your schools, said very kindly to me that she'd noticed that we English people speak with precision in our words; that we are careful to use words, she thought, in their exact meaning. And while that was too kind of her to say so, we do so try to speak. And I think I would like to say to you now that we do not normally confuse, as is sometimes confused, the words "joy" and "pleasure." People often use them as though they are synonyms, as though they meant the same thing. They don't! They don't! It's important to my purpose now to explain the difference. If I was to speak from this chair: pleasures come and go. The things that give you pleasure change in every period of your life. Everybody, in this auditorium this evening, could write his or her autobiography around the different things that have given you pleasure at different times, and they've been changing all your life.

When I was a little boy—I insist that I was a very little boy, and this is true—my pleasure depended upon what was on the table. Some of the men in front are trying to look superior as though that was never true of them. I don't believe it. Time was, with all of us, when our pleasure, I fancy, depended on what was on the table. For me it was potato crisps, merengue and ice cream. Does it pass? I grew out of that but even as a small boy at school I still retained a taste for chocolate. I did like chocolate. My pleasure depended, as a small boy, on chocolate. Indeed, my favourite dream was of an endless bar of chocolate being pressed by an unseen hand into my ever-open mouth.

I got over it. I've not really been interested in chocolate, not really for a long time. I only eat chocolate when I buy it for my wife. She wonders who I bought it for. And then, that was succeeded in my little life by that passion which I described to you this morning,[10] which all English boys have: they reach the age when they must have a bicycle. Then they work on dad to get a bicycle. Oh, I worked on my father. He didn't want me to have it—but I got it. I wore him down! I gave five shillings for it. That's a good deal less than a dollar. I bought it from my elder brother. If you had seen the bicycle you would have said it was dear. Oh, but the bliss I had in riding round the block. That was my pleasure at my age of eleven. I only get on a bicycle now when I must. It's gone.

---

10. This sermon follows "How to Covet," which was delivered in the morning.

All life is like that. The games have changed, the interests change. It is the nature of pleasure they change with changing years. Wholesome and good, many of them, but they're fugitives; they belong to different ages of your life.

The joy—whenever we think of joy, and this deep joy in Jesus—it springs and springs again. It need never go. It came to my heart as a boy of thirteen when I said "Yes" to Jesus in my heart and it has never left me.[11] Never! Sometimes it flames into rapture and sometimes it sinks into peace but the difference he made—it doesn't change. It can be in the heart of a boy at the high school. It can be in the heart of a young man at business, the undergraduate at the university, all through life. In the grim days of the First World War I had it still.[12] In the grim days of the Second World War, when my dear wife and I lived, as I think I told you once, in public air raid shelters for five years and a month, used great curtains, when we were in those, to cover us on the floor and said to the survivors of decimated families, "Come in, we'll offer you a home here." And we slept together and we prayed together. Half a million of them passed through our home in that five years and a month.[13] And every night I had to go from shelter to shelter to look after the other people. And many of the great buildings through London I saw fold up before my eyes and I felt many a night, "It must be my turn now. I can't always be missed. I'd been missed so narrowly and so often. It must be my turn." Many a time I had opportunity to pick up my heart as I looked death quietly in the face and asked myself, "Is it all right now? Now is it all right? Is it still there; that peace in Jesus, that joy of the Lord?" And it was still there.

Mr. Ghandi was right. Mr. Ghandi said nobody has really mastered life till he's looked death quietly in the face.[14] We have been forced to look death

11. Sangster experienced a personal conversion aged thirteen on October 19, 1913 at Radnor Street Mission. See Cheatle, *W. E. Sangster - Herald of Holiness*, 3. Paul Sangster records his father's own words. After being asked whether he wished to give his heart to Christ, by his Sunday school teacher, Sangster recalls the event: "I hesitated a little. I did—and I didn't. Half of me was eager and half afraid. I think my chief hesitancy turned on 'whether I could keep it up' . . . The best part of me won. 'I think I do,' I faltered. He led me into another room and knelt with me in prayer. He prayed *with* me and *for* me, and invited me to pray myself. I spluttered out a little prayer. It had one merit. I *meant* it. That day I handed over my life to Christ . . ." P. Sangster, *Doctor Sangster*, 33.

12. Sangster was posted to Germany in the aftermath of WWI, leaving on March 29, 1919 and returning to England around Christmastime 1919. P. Sangster, *Doctor Sangster*, 44–47.

13. An article giving details about the time and ministry in the shelters and Sangster's role is given in the article "When London Methodism Went Underground," *Methodist Recorder*, June 14, 1945, 3. The author is in personal possession of a letter detailing the layout and daily life of the Sangster's during the war years within the Westminster Central Hall air raid shelter. See also P. Sangster, *Doctor Sangster*, 189–202.

14. Mahatma Gandhi (1869–1948), Indian civil rights leader who came to prominence

quietly in the face, to have lived with it and never expected to survive. But He brought us through. He was close to us in the experiences of the dark and when walking about with the bombs singing around your ears. He's still there and He's still precious. We say to people who are looking for what they call a "[gemmed][15] life," for a kick out of life, for this and that, we say to them, "The place of joy is in Jesus. If you want it, go to the corner of the street. Go into that church of God. And if they know their business they'll give you the secret of joy."

My friends, I am going to be bold tonight. You see, I feel so at home with you here at Junaluska. And as my dear wife has told you, you are so much in our conversation in London. And one can take liberties with friends. As an Englishmen, as an Englishmen you see it, when you come to your country from ours, and we are amazed at the wonderful things you have. Quite wonderful, all the things, perfectly abound. What wonderful refrigerators, and some of you change them so often, don't you? Your cars, sometimes more cars than one in a family. In one family, more cars than one. And washing machines that we were speaking about this morning,[16] and this and that, and little buttons to press. Isn't it wonderful. We stand amazed. We crawl into our room at night and we say, "Oh, the wonderful things our friends have." And we are so glad for them because they work hard and they are so good and kind to others. But that's how you impress us: the wonderful things in your wonderful country. One of the things that has astonished me most is your car dumps. Oh, how I wander around your car dumps. If anybody can tell me of a dump for cars, you know when you toss them away, when they are of no use, anywhere near Lake Junaluska, I shall be in danger of missing an appointment. I would love to go and see those car dumps. It's perfectly clear to me that you toss cars on the dump at precisely the condition at which a Methodist minister in England could begin to be interested in a car.

But we've been noticing something else as well. You see, among other things I am an author and I write books, and when you write books you're interested in other people's books, and I can't easily pass a bookshop. So, amazed at all the wonderful things in your wonderful country, I've been going in the

---

as the mystic leader of the Independent Movement against British rule, famed for employing non-violent civil disobedience. Gandhi's legacy was primarily to lead India to independence from the British Empire and as a consequence inspiring future movements for civil rights and freedom across the world, based on non-violent demonstration. Assassinated on January 30, 1948 by a young Hindu, though speculation was rife about who was really behind the killing. Brown, "Gandhi, Mohandas Karamchand [Mahatma Gandhi] (1869–1948)," *ODNB*.

15. Inaudible.

16. See the sermon "How to Covet."

bookshops as well, in New York, Ocean City, other places we've been. And I've been seeing the popular books, the best-sellers, and I've been astonished to find how many best-sellers are all about how to be happy. How to be happy, yes! I've got some of the titles, notice: *Peace of Mind*.[17] Washers, cars, refrigerators, and one of the best-sellers, *Peace of Mind. Live Longer, Look Younger*. Oh, what a title.[18] I had to steer my wife past that. I was afraid she would be taking a few more dollars from me when she saw *Live Longer, Look Younger. How to Make Friends and Influence People*.[19] We met a lady in London some time ago that said she got a hold of a copy of that book and she studied it and she'd lost all her friends. Now, I've not studied the book so I don't know, but she said that somewhere in the book it told you at a certain point in the conversation to rest your chin in the cup of your right hand, lean forward, and as she leaned forward to her friends they all retreated. Anyhow, don't you worry about her; she's thrown the book away and she's got her friends back.

My dear friends, what I'm asking you to notice—and observe the impertinence of an old friend in doing this, because everybody who knows me knows how much I love honestly America. I'm just putting it to you with the intimacy and frankness that a friend may. We come, and we see these wonderful things and they seem to be shared—all kinds of people have them—and then we go into the book shops and so many of these best-sellers are about how to be happy. Oh, fancy, fancy having three cars even, and two refrigerators and a couple of washing machines, and having to sit on the porch reading a book on how to be happy.

Listen, I believed it because my Lord said it to me long ago. Jesus said, "A man's life consisteth not in the abundance of the things which he possesses" [Luke 12:15]. And now I've seen that. I know it's true, because nowhere in this wide world is there a nation that has your standard of living—nowhere. And I don't begrudge it to you. God bless you. I'm glad you have it. I can be glad for you. Nowhere is there such a standard of living and at the same time with all these amazing things some of your fellow countrymen—not you, not you, but some of your fellow countrymen with all these things—are reading books on how to be happy. So it proves it, it confirms the Divine word again, "A man's life consisteth not in the abundance of the things that he possesses." And, if it's joy you want, it isn't in a line of cars and refrigerators and this and that and

17. Leibman, *Peace of Mind*.

18. The book he is referring to was Hauser, *Look Younger, Live Longer*, on the New York bestseller list for a year. His next book could also have caught Sangster's attention: *Be Happier, Be Healthier* (1952).

19. The book he is referring to was the bestseller by Dale Carnegie, *How to Win Friends and Influence People* (1936). Another of his self-help books which would have been in circulation when Sangster was in the US was *How to Stop Worrying and Start Living* (1948).

more buttons to press. It's whether or not you really have Jesus in your heart, whether your sins have been forgiven, and you know it, and you're learning how to open yourself more and more to him, and can wake every morning and feel, "Lord, another day with thee." There's the spring of joy. You people who come to Junaluska, you know it. That it's clear that there are some of your fellow countrymen who do not know it.

Oh, I beg you—I have a right to say this a visitor may—I beg you: heed the pleaded of your number that lead you in evangelism. Heed their words, consider their programmes. Go back to your own towns convinced of this: that if people are to make sense of life and find the secret of joy, it will depend on you. And if you fail in your church, some of them—awful thought—may go all their days unblessed. Whenever this religion of ours breaks fresh from the rock, it always breaks fresh with this note of exuberant joy in it. It's when religion is getting chill that it gets so correct and straight laced, and afraid to smile, and more concerned about ritual than it's concerned about anything else. But when this faith breaks fresh from the rock, always it has this note of exuberant joy in it. It did at Pentecost [Acts 2]. We all know the apostles on the day of Pentecost were suspected of being drunk. People said, looking at those shining exuberant, joy filled men, people said, "They're filled with new wine" [Acts 2:13]. Maybe you've never been suspected of being drunk for as good reasons as that. It isn't a compliment. Saint Francis, if you remember, had to reprove his followers once. Why did he have to reprove them? Because they laughed in church he reproved them. And they said to him afterwards, "Brother Francis, we can't help it. We are so happy."[20] The early Methodists set their hymns, some of their early hymns, to dance tunes.[21] They did. It shocked the eighteenth century in England. It shocked them because we are very correct over there, and as my wife has said, "very reserved," and for people to come forward and put their hymns to dance tunes shocked the nation:

> My God I am thine, what a comfort divine,
> what a blessing to know that my Jesus is mine.
> In the heavenly lamb thrice happy I am,
> and my heart it does dance at the sound of his name.[22]

20. Sangster was very likely reliant on the account of the life St. Francis by Johannes Jørgensen, *Saint Francis of Assisi*, which also details the actions of his followers. Sangster used this source in his research for his book *The Pure in Heart*, written just two years prior to the World Methodist Conference..

21. See *CHPCM*.

22. The first verse of Charles Wesley's hymn "My God, I Am Thine; What a Comfort Divine," in *CHPCM*, 328.

And their feet went with their hearts. They couldn't help it. They were so happy.

So it was with the early Salvationists who have been mentioned already this evening. Those early Salvationists, they had it. Whenever the faith breaks fresh, I say, from the rock it has this note of exuberant joy in it. You've all heard the story, but you don't know where it really happened and I do. It was Doctor Farmer who was organist at Harrow School who told the story first.[23] Harrow, the school to which Winston Churchill went. Doctor Farmer, their organist, was ask to adjudicate once at a band festival, and a Salvation Army band was competing. Now, I think Dr. Farmer wanted the Salvationists to win. I think he did. But he did something that was rather unethical in an adjudicator. In the interval he slipped down to give the Salvationists some advice. He said—you remember the story—to the man with the big drum; he whispered to him, he said, "My good fellow, need you knock that drum so hard?" And the beaming bandsman replied to Dr. Farmer, "No, Sir, I'm that happy I could bust the blooming drum." How strange it seems to us. How superior you feel. I do too but I don't feel as superior as you do. No.

William Booth, the founder of the Salvation Army, would interrupt his speeches sometimes, carried away with the rapture of the faith, and he'd say to his soldiers, "I'm so happy I want to jump for joy. Will you all stand up and jump with me?" So they'd all stand up, jump, sit down, and he'd go on with the speech. I know what you all thinking. I hope this fellow from England doesn't make that suggestion to us this evening. It's all right, I'm not going to. I'm only going to say this to you: I understand what moved the old man; the wonder, the joy of Jesus. Some of you will be saying, "But does this joy, that flames, you say, at times into rapture and sinks at other times into peace, does it abide with us always? Can it? Can it in sickness and in difficulty?" It can. In advanced souls it can.

I visit a woman in Chelsea twisted with arthritis. She lives in one little room, a front room. She can see what's happening in the mean little street. When I go to see her I press the bell, and then I wait five minutes. She's only just there. I can see her through the window. She's only got to go like that[24] and open the door but I wait five minutes. It takes her all that time to come. It takes her a full minute to stand up. She has almost to unlock herself and then with pain she edges her way to the door and lets me in. And then it's another

23. John Farmer (1835–1901), British musician, composer and prestigious organist. Was organ teacher at Harrow School between 1862 and 1885 before serving at Balliol College, Oxford as organist until his death. Farmer's enthusiastic personality made him popular beyond his formal employment and he was a great supporter of communal singing and musical education, travelling to other leading schools and colleges to lecture, conduct and examine. Walker, "Farmer, John (1835–1901)," *ODNB*.

24. Likely referring to a gesture.

five minutes getting back to her chair again. Then we talk—I mean, she talks. Oh yes, the minister is always glad when you do the talking when he calls. To be a good preacher you must be a good speaker but to be a good pastor you must be a good listener. We're happy to get you talking. Some of you don't want much encouragement either. Dear Mrs. Atkinson, how she talks, and it's all about the goodness of God. "O Doctor," she says, "I just sit her amazed at the goodness of God to me. It might have been a backroom and I couldn't see anything but a dirty yard. It's a front room and I can see everything that's happening on the street. Oh, my neighbour's husband, he's a good fellow. Do you know he's made a little thing so that I can turn over the pages of my book, just with my two fingers?" The only way she could turn them over. She said, "And this hot meal service, isn't it wonderful? Five days a week they bring me a hot meal to the door." And so she goes on, and on, and on about the goodness of God. And the peace of God is in her. And his joy lights up her face. And when I go home I know she's done me more good than I've done her. And I go into the house and I say to my wife, "Isn't life wonderful? I can do this."[25] And she laughs and says, "Ah, my dear, I know where you've been," Isn't life wonderful when you can do that? Mrs. Atkinson can't do it. Not a finger can she move. The joy of Jesus is in her still. Death, just as with her sister, will come in God's good time to conduct her to his more immediate presence. But she's half living in heaven as it is. She is.

My friend, the joy of life—they're looking for it everywhere. They're seeking it in things, things, and more things. And it isn't in things. And it isn't in many of the books that propound the idea of getting it. Oh no. It's in our Lord! And it can be found in his church.

Here's the sermon's briefest thing I want to say to you. First, when we answer the question, "What is the church for?," we say, "It makes sense of life. It gives joy to life." We say this finally: "It puts purpose in life." You know human nature is so made—God made us this way—human nature is so made that it is never satisfied to live. It wants something to live for. And one of the most embarrassing questions you can put to non-Christians is this: "What are you living for?" I have often embarrassed people by that question, "What are you living for?" The more honest of them say, "I'm living for myself." And that's one of the reasons why this earth looks sometimes like hell.

I know a man in England who received a letter some time ago from a solicitor. I don't know what solicitor's letters are like in America, but in England when a solicitor has a bit of good news to give you he doesn't hurry to give it to you. He's as reserved over that as he is over everything else. And they've got a technical phrase, have our lawyers, to intimate that somebody's

25. Likely referring to a hand gesture.

mentioned you in their will. Now you know why I've never received one of these letters, but let that go. This man received a letter from the lawyer saying, "Would he prove his identity. Would he confirm the fact that he was so and so, and if he would, he would hear something to his advantage." That's the phrase. Isn't it a nice phrase? I've often wondered what the feeling must be when you read that: "You will hear something to your advantage." Well, he was a Yorkshireman. I told you a bit about Yorkshiremen last evening. They're dour. They're slow. He didn't permit himself to get excited until he knew how much he was going to hear to his advantage. But when he heard, and it was a thumping big sum, oh, he was so happy. Oh, he was so happy. You know why he was so happy? Because he wouldn't have to work anymore. What a lovely thought: "I won't have to work anymore." Well, he bought a house in the country, got a nice garden and a gardener to look after it. And I think I can give you a typical day in his life.

He gets up in the morning, not very early, and he eats a little bit of bacon. He reads the paper and then goes out into the garden to smell the morning. And then he comes back again and has an early lunch. If the weather is suitable he goes after lunch to play a game of golf. He returns after the golf to a cup of tea. He has dinner in the evening at 7:00. Before he was left a fortune he always had his dinner at 1:00, but now he has it at 7:00 in the evening. And he spends the evening playing bridge or looking at TV. And not very late he goes to bed, and tomorrow morning, not very early, he will rise again. He will eat a little bit of bacon, go out and smell the morning. A friend of mine was staying with him the other day and told me about it. And I said to my friend—and you know my friend by name—I said, "Leslie, what did you to him?[26] We have duties to men like that. What's he living for?" And Leslie said, "Well, a bit difficult when a fellow is your host, but I did try to draw him out. I said to him, 'Why do you play golf?' And he said, 'To keep fit.' So, I said to him, 'What are you keeping fit for?' So, he had a longer think over that and then he said, 'Oh, to play more

---

26. Leslie Dixon Weatherhead, CBE (1893–1976), British Methodist minister renowned for his utilisation of psychology in his ministry and many writings. Weatherhead was a popular and internationally acclaimed preacher famed for his eloquent tongue and seraphic voice. During the 1940s and 50s it became common for visitors to London to go and hear Weatherhead for one Sunday service at the City Temple and Sangster at Westminster for the other, both attracting huge crowds to their churches. He was an author of numerous books combining Christian ideas of the gospel with the insights of psychology. He became president of the British Methodist Conference in 1955 and the first British Methodist minister to be awarded the CBE. Travell, *Doctor of Souls*.

Weatherhead and Sangster were great friends, both becoming presidents of the British Methodist Conference. Weatherhead wrote a short biography of Sangster as he prepared to occupy the President's chair, in *Methodist Recorder*, July 13, 1950, 9.

golf.'" The madness of it. Men born and built to the scale of eternity, sent into the world to do things for God, and that's what they are doing.

What lovely fellowship we've had with that good man that has now left us. I speak more freely now I know he isn't here. In his seventies, Doctor Laubach [. . .][27] was like John Wesley, who takes the world as his parish, his suit of influence. My dear friends: the zest for living. Does anybody ever ask him what he's living for? Nobody, I trust, of intelligence will ever ask you because you are so obviously drawn out in the service of God. Busy to old age even for him; retired maybe, but not of the strength; doing what he wants him to do; commending your Lord by your prayers, by your personal witness, seeking to do all you can with a purpose in life. If there are people sick of life because they have no purpose, you're not of their number. So you, as Christians, have the greatest purpose of all.

What is the church for? It makes sense of life. It gives joy to life. It puts purpose into life. That and much else. Serve, my dear friends, your Lord, through his church.

Let us pray.

Almighty God,
If we have been indifferent of thy church;
if we have been cold Christians;
if we have even thought that happiness depended in things;
Oh, disabuse our minds this evening.
Endue us this very evening to a still deeper consecration.
For thy name's sake.

Amen.

27. The tape is damaged here and a very short section is missing on what appears to be a reference to what Frank Laubach did in his seventies. It would seem by the context that Sangster would have been referring to "Laubach Literacy," which he founded in 1955 to help address the worldwide problem of illiteracy. "Dr. Laubach believed that literacy was the 'first step toward ending the suffering and exploitation of the world's disadvantaged people.'" Laubach Literacy International Records, http://library.syr.edu/digital/guides/l/laubach_lit.htm.

CHAPTER 10

Called to Be Saints[1]

Called to be saints. Called to be saints. [Rom 1:7]

THE WORD "SAINT" TODAY is used with a great variety of meaning. Sometimes it is used satirically by worldlings when they seek to excuse their sins and say, "I'm no saint!" Sometimes it's used cheaply by people who try to reduce our glorious gospel to a little mild morality, and who will say of anybody who doesn't tell suggestive stories and keeps out of the hands of the police, "He's a saint!" Sometimes it is used negatively by those lopsided kind of puritans who think our glorious gospel is a series of negations and who will say of some of their acquaintances, "He doesn't drink; he doesn't smoke; he doesn't bet; he doesn't joke. He's a saint!" And sometimes the word is used with what I could call a kind of high austerity, as by the leaders of the Roman Church and the Greek Church when they say, "This term is so high. You musn't use it loosely. The church must decide who should be called saints. We'll canonise them, and then tell you of whom this august term may be employed." And they use it of men and women of such rare virtue that it's only given about a dozen times a century.

But what we're concerned, this evening, to decide, as Bible students, is what the Bible means by the word "saint." And most particularly what it means in the New Testament and, with greatest particularity of all, what St.

---

1. This sermon was preached on September 9, 1956 at the second Sunday evening service of the World Methodist Conference in Junaluska. The theme for the whole conference was "Methodism in the Contemporary World."

A very different version of this sermon is found in the addresses section of Clark and Perkins, eds., *Proceedings of the Ninth World Methodist Conference*, 358–65. The present version is a transcript directly from a sound recording of his preaching, therefore, presenting for the first time an unedited version of exactly what Sangster preached. A comparison of the two versions is of great value for scholars of homiletics wishing to gain a sense of how Sangster either edited his sermons for publication or adapted the verbal act of preaching from more formal manuscripts.

Paul meant when he said to the Christians in Rome, "You're called, you're called to be saints" [Rom 1:7].

Now my dear friends, in the New Testament the word "saint" is used of anybody who has received the Holy Spirit and in whom Christ is being formed afresh. Let me say it again: in the New Testament the word "saint" is used of anyone who has really received the Holy Spirit, and in whom Christ is being formed afresh.[2] And the moment you get that definition sharp in your mind, you see the deficiencies of the other definitions. The satire of worldlings is seen for the blasphemous thing that it is. What do they know about the indwelling of the Holy Spirit? The mild morality that would cheapen the term, and the lopsided puritanism that would see it only as a series of negations—even that we can brush aside. This glorious religion of ours is not less and less but more and more. It's not chopping off, it's not filleting our personalities. It is that gospel concerning which St. Paul said, "All things are yours" [1 Cor 3:21]. And even the high-austere use of this term by the Roman and the Greek Churches is seen to be a more restricted use of it than the New Testament would allow. Not all the saints in Rome, in Jerusalem, in Philippi had scaled the heights of holiness. Not all of them, but they had all received the Holy Spirit. And Christ was being formed afresh in them, and in glorious anticipation of was yet to be. In loving certitude of what God was doing with them, Paul used the word "saint" of them, said, "Saints in Jerusalem, saints in Philippi, saints in Ephesus, saints in Colossae." And everywhere the Christians are "called to be saints."[3]

We are still called! It is one of the tragic differences between modern Methodism and early Methodism that we do not so clearly hear the call.

My friends, however far we may be ourselves from this quality of life, I'm going to be bold this evening and assume that you all know what I'm talking about. This quality of life lingers in Methodism like a lovely fragrance. There isn't one among you that doesn't remember somebody who enjoyed it. Was it some old minister of God you knew, some local preacher, some class leader? Was it your old mother who had it? But there isn't anybody here, I judge, who hasn't known at some time or other some soul who had this quality of life. You know what I mean. The "earthly part of them glowed with the fire divine."[4] Supernatural love streamed out of them. The peace of God dwelt in them. They were good, and good in the inward parts.[5] They were not censorious, critical of other people. When they can't say anything

2. Sangster had discussed this viewpoint in some depth in *The Pure in Heart*, 27–42.

3. E.g., Rom 1:7; 1 Cor 1:2; Eph 1:1; Phil 1:1; Col 1:2.

4. Final two lines of the third stanza of "Breathe on Me Breathe of God," by Edwin Hatch (1835–89).

5. An allusion to Ps 51:6.

good about you, they're dumb. You know your reputation is always safe in their hands. They remind you, without knowing it, they remind you of Jesus. And through the years their memory almost haunts you and in your best moments you want to be like them.

You've all known this quality of life. In some others, you have known it. If it isn't as common among us as once it was, and I do not think it is, you have all seen it. The thing holds you and draws you and haunts you. And to that quality of life, I remind you, as this solemn conference draws on to its close, that you are all called.

Those who possessed it were not necessarily educated people, though some were. You'll find it more often among the poor than the rich. They are not dominant personalities and yet somehow or other when they come into the room you can't overlook them. This is the kind of life we're needing. This is the kind of life possible to us. I believe this kind of life could be found in all communions, but I hope nobody here will think it is denominational bias on my part when I say that I think that time was when it was common, common in early Methodism, when God—who knows his saint, for he makes them at the last; only he knows them—when God could have numbered them among us by the thousands. This, as so many of you know, was the great central teaching that John Wesley had. He opened his own heart to it as a young man of twenty-three.[6] He came better to understand it as a man of thirty-five.[7] But he went on preaching it till he was eighty-eight, and died preaching it.[8] He said, "Salvation is not enough." He said, "Even salvation isn't full salvation unless it is sanctification as well." He said, "Where this is preached Methodism will flourish, where this is rejected Methodism will languish."[9] It was obsessional with him. Was it indeed a magnificent obsession? Had he the very heart of the gospel in this teaching? I believe he had.

---

6. Wesley, *Plain Account of Christian Perfection*, 9–10.

7. It seems most likely that Sangster is referring here to John Wesley's experience of May 24, 1738 at Aldersgate Street, though more contemporary studies of John Wesley would see much of 1738 as being a time of personal reflection and gradual reordering of his faith and theology.

8. The importance of holiness, particularly imparted holiness, continued to be John Wesley's most characteristic emphasis in his sermons until his death in 1791. "On a Single Eye," now dated by Wesley scholars to 1790, is probably the most focused and clear expression of his late views on the subject of holiness of heart. Sangster's editions of John Wesley's sermons (Jackson) would have dated this to 1761.

9. A common quote attributed to John Wesley, which is probably an amalgamation of various statements but does not exist in these words.

I want to make three affirmations, here this evening, about the early Methodist people. And I want to glance at each of them in turn. I'm going to say this:

They saw the goal.

They knew the way.

They reached the heights.

Charles Wesley, who could always turn his brother's teaching into song, he wrote scores of hymns for those rejoicing Christians to use, and this among them:

> Give me a new, a perfect heart,
> From doubt, and fear, and sorrow free;
> The mind which was in Christ impart,
> And let my spirit cleave to Thee.[10]

Each in turn, then. Let us look at my affirmations. Let us examine them honestly and in humility and see if we can truly believe that this was the fact concerning our spiritual forebears:

They saw the goal.

They knew the way.

They reached the heights.

I say first that they saw the goal. My friends, there are many Christians today in our churches who do not see the goal, who accept a lower standard of Christian conduct for themselves and for their fellows than the New Testament teaches as normal. There is no lack, alas, of people in our churches who are censorious, and jealous, and proud, and selfish, and thrustful. We see them in our churches. God forgive us. We see them in our looking glasses.

In a church in the suburbs of London some few months ago, in a Methodist church, a young married woman came in. She seemed so eager, and the minister was so glad. She came and settled down among the people. She stayed for three months. And then she left. And the minister sought her out and said, "You're not coming again?" And she said, "No!" And he said, "Has anybody been unkind to you?" And she said:

> Oh no! They've been most kind to me but when I got among them,
> when I was intimate enough to be allowed to help the women
> preparing the socials and other things, when I got into the con-
> versations behind the scenes, I found that they were as critical of

---

10. From Charles Wesley's hymn "God of All Power, and Truth, and Grace." There were originally twenty-eight stanzas. This particular stanza is not in the 1780 *CHPCM* (553–54). The whole hymn can be found at the end of John Wesley's Sermon 40, "On Christian Perfection," in *CHPCM*, 553, n. 380.

other people as people are in the world. I found them as touchy, as pushing, as eager to be first. I thought you people had the secret of life the rest of us haven't got. I was mistaken.

My friends, would that be true of any church that you know? Would it indeed?

There are many people, I say, in our churches who are living on a sub-Christian standard. Some of them don't know it and some of them know it and defend it. They say, "My circumstances are peculiar. This is a very busy and modern world. You can't expect us to live as they lived in New Testament times." They blame their circumstances, forgetting that there were saints in Caesar's household, and that Caesar was Nero, that bloodstained and inhuman monster. Whose circumstances could have been worse than theirs? Or they say, "I know that's true of me. It's my temperament. I have that kind of temper, that kind of temperament." And when they use "temperament" in that sense they mean "temper too old to spank!" They excuse it on the ground of their temperament. Or, sometimes they say it was their inheritance. "I know I'm like this, but so was my father. You see, I take after my father." And so they defend it! They don't even admit the obligation! They don't say, "We're called to be saints!" They know they're living on this lower level than they need and they excuse themselves. They think the grace of God is defeated by your circumstances, or your temperament, or your inheritance.

Our spiritual forbears, they never did that. They slipped on the way but they never denied the obligation. They said, "We're called to be saints." Ever the goal was in view. When their Calvinistic opponents in the eighteenth century said to them, "Oh yes, Christ saves us *in* sinning," they said, "Yes, but *from* sinning as well." When their Calvinistic opponents said, "God can't do anything else with sin but cancel it," they said, "Yes! Yes! 'He breaks the power of cancelled sin. And sets the prisoner free.'"[11] They knew what they believed and that they were called to be saints. They sang, as their great hymn writer taught them to sing:

> He wills that I should holy be;
> That holiness I long to feel,
> That full divine conformity
> To all my Saviour's righteous will.[12]

So I ask you my dear friends, as I ask myself, do we see the goal as clearly as they did? Do we obviously and plainly admit the obligation? I can't deny

11. From the first two lines of the fourth stanza of Charles Wesley's hymn "O for a Thousand Tongues to Sing," in *CHPCM*, 79–80.

12. The first stanza of Charles Wesley's hymn "He Wills That I Should Holy Be," in *CHPCM*, 572.

it. I'm not there but I admit the obligation. If St. Paul came among us at this great Methodist conference, would he know us as his own? Or, would he be as perplexed as it seemed he was when he once went to Ephesus and found a worshiping group who were seriously deficient somewhere. And having watched them for a bit, he said, "Did you receive the Holy Ghost when ye believed? And they had not so much as heard that the Holy Ghost was given" [Acts 19:1–7]. We've heard. And if some of the speeches at our conference are to be believed, as I believe those penetrating minds are, we've heard. But we've almost forgotten. That first: they saw the goal!

This secondly: they knew the way. You see, it was common knowledge among those early Methodists that they had been saved by grace through faith.[13] Their descendants may have become nebulous in their theology and confused the gospel with its strong dogmatic heart, with a little uplift, so that an American editor, as we have been reminded, can write a leader in his paper and say of our great communion, "They're busy in good works but they're short on theology."[14] We may have lost our theology on the way. It may have become with us—God forgive us, if it has—what I called in a group the other morning, "a gelatinous mass of vague sentiment." But these our forebears, they knew that their gospel had a strong dogmatic heart. And among other things they knew this: that they were saved by grace through faith.[15] This was their peculiarity in this pursuit of holiness: that they carried over the same divine agency into sanctification as well. They said, "If grace can use faith to save us, cannot grace use faith also to sanctify us? Did God intend it?" They searched the Scriptures. They found the promise there. They dwelt on texts like these: "He which began a good work in you will perfect it until the day of Jesus Christ" [Phil 1:6]; "He which began a good work in us will perfect it" [Phil 1:6]. Did he say that? The one who left the lap of the world against the man who started to build and had not the wherewith to finish, he won't fall into the same condemnation. "He which began a good work in you, will perfect it until the day of Jesus Christ" [Phil 1:6]. And when they were sure God had promised to do this—to lift the quality of our living to a level the world does not know—when they were sure

---

13. Eph 2:8.

14. While it has not been possible to locate this quotation in the published versions of the addresses in the *Proceedings*, the only address which does speak about Methodism and this perception of its theology was given by the Methodist Reformation scholar Gordon Rupp on Friday Sept 7, 1956 in the early evening lecture, just two days before Sangster's sermon. Rupp, "Methodism in Relation to the Protestant World," in Clark and Perkins, eds., *Proceedings*, 24, 295–306.

15. Eph 2:8.

of it, they claimed it. And they claimed it by faith. They sent faith before to grasp it, till faith was lost in sight.[16] They said:

> Faith, mighty faith, the promise sees,
> And looks to that alone,
> Laughs at impossibilities,
> And cries: It shall be done![17]

And listen what they did: they believed for holiness. They—observe it—they didn't think holiness was an achievement, as some of us still think. They knew it was a gift. They knew they couldn't do it. They knew this was an agency of the Holy Spirit, that faith opened them to it. And so they believed for it. They turned the word "belief" into a militant noun. It was "faith," booted, spurred and mounted. They said, "In Jesus, I believe and will believe myself for him." So, "drawn by the lure of strong desire, the Holy Spirit came and sanctified their breath."[18]

Now my friends, I would like to point out to you that this isn't as stupid as it seems—not as stupid as it seems to Quiller Couch, who my friend Dr. Maldwyn Edwards quoted from this desk a week ago tonight.[19] Quiller Couch said in his book on Hetty Wesley, "To believe and to have, what nonsense!"[20] Nonsense to him, not nonsense to these believing souls. And I ask you to observe this: that the modern psychologist is coming to say they were right—not that I feel I need the modern psychologist to reinforce their testimony. I should believe in it just as well if they didn't believe in it. But it interests me to notice that he's catching up. Now my friends, the modern psychologist says this in giving practical counsel to people who want to improve in any way, that want to reach a certain aim, the modern psychologist says this: "You must have your aim clear in mind. No vagueness. Give it sharp edges. You must have your aim clear in mind." They had it clear in mind. They looked to Jesus and they longed to have him formed afresh in them. And the modern psychologist says this to do: "Now you must warm it with desire. You must long for it." They longed for it. They longed for it above

---

16. Final line of the fourth stanza of Augustus Toplady's (1740–78) hymn "Father Creator of Mankind."

17. The ninth stanza of Charles Wesley's hymn "Father of Jesus Christ, My Lord," in *CHPCM*, 515–16.

18. The third and fourth lines of the first stanza of Charles Wesley's hymn "Come, Holy Ghost, All-Quick'ning Fire," in *CHPCM*, 532–33.

19. This message was delivered at the first Sunday evening service of the conference. See Edwards, "Wesley Family," in Clark and Perkins, eds., *Proceedings*, 116–22 (118).

20. Quiller-Couch, *Hetty Wesley*, viii.

everything else. This is what they wanted more than any worldly advancement. They longed for it. Then, says the modern psychologist, "You must use imagination. You must see the thing you're seeking actually done. See it in the eye of imagination and imagination will come down like a great crane and lift you from what you are to what you could be."

And we all know the catch in that because at its basis it's really auto-suggestion and it's often kidding yourself to believe what isn't true.[21] But our spiritual forebears didn't make that mistake. They held it within their minds; they held it warm in their believing hearts; they had faith for the thing. They saw it done! And then their faith opened them, opened them to the thing—the modern psychologist leads us—to all the agencies of the Holy Spirit just as God promised. And the Holy Spirit came in and did it. And they walked about among their fellows, alight with the light of heaven, good in the inward parts. They made Methodism mighty. Why did it spread like a prairie fire through England? Why did it overleap the Atlantic and spread throughout the world? Because we could sing better or preach better? No! The great "impossible" was the Holy Spirit. And the proof that he was in his people was in their amazing and transformed lives. And they lived like that. Listen, they lived like that easily. By which I mean it wasn't toiling self-effort; that they weren't screwed up and doing it themselves. They didn't belong to that class of people that I described here the other day as "living on their nerves and getting on other people's." They weren't doing it themselves. It was an agency of the Holy Ghost. And people looked on them and saw their seraphic faces and knew that God had moved among his people again.

Oh, how different we are now. What academics we have; how we can dress up; and when we are in our full glory, like we were last Sunday, not even Solomon in all his glory was arrayed like some of us.[22] They hadn't so many things that we have but they had this: they had God living in them, the Holy Ghost resident in their soul, "the life of God in the soul of man,"[23] and Jesus being formed afresh in them. Paul would have known them. He would have done. He wouldn't have said, "Did you receive the Holy Ghost when ye believed?" [Acts 19:1-7]. So, they believed for it. They knew what the hardest thing of all was to believe: to believe that they could ever have the mastery of sin. Charles Wesley said:

21. Autosuggestion was a psychological technique that was developed by pharmacist and psychologist Émile Coué (1857–1926) in the early twentieth century, publishing his work in England in 1920. Coué, *Self-Mastery Through Conscious Autosuggestion*.

22. Sangster is referring to the 11:00 a.m. processional service on September 2, 1956 in which people were robed. The sermon was delivered by Dr. Harold Roberts, vice president of the World Methodist Conference. Clark and Perkins, eds., *Proceedings*, 21.

23. *The Life of God in the Soul of Man*, op. cit.

> The most impossible of all
> Is that I ere from sin should cease;
> Yet shall it be, I know it shall.

Now listen to this impertinent line:

> Jesus, look to thy faithfulness!
> If nothing is too hard for Thee
> All things are possible to me'[24]

I say they knew the way. By grace they had been saved through faith. By grace they would be sanctified as well.

This thirdly: they reached the heights. They saw the goal. They knew the way. They reached the heights. Now I half suspect that there are those among you, this evening, who really wonder if I'm exaggerating all this. You will begin to think whether it ever happened. You will be reminded yourself that it is a common bias of the human mind to idealise the past. And you will be saying to yourself, "And that's what this preacher from England is doing. He's idealising the past." I wish I could agree with you. My conscience would be easier if I could. I can't. Believe me, this happened. They were true life—make terms with that. They had that quality of life. It happened. You're here because they had it. But you won't stay here unless you recover it. And if I may select one illustration of this to leave you in no doubt about it at all, I will mention a man whose name has only had one mention this week, as far as I know, and I sat close to this conference; just one passing mention he's had and he deserves more than that. I mean John Fletcher of Madeley, that great saint of early Methodism, John Wesley's own designated successor. Wesley said, "When I die let John Fletcher of Madeley be the leader of the Methodist people."[25] But he predeceased John Wesley and never came to the succession. But that great, that holy man, let him stand. And I'm saying this, as I begin in quoting him to you. I want you to understand, he wasn't unique. He wasn't even rare. He came to notice because of his writings and because Wesley designated him as his successor.[26] But he was not rare! There were thousands, thousands like him in early Methodism. But let him serve to illustrate this quality of life that our people had and we, alas, I fear have mislaid.

Remember what non-Methodists said about him. Dr. Frank Baker quoted Southey the other day. Listen to Southey on Fletcher—not a Methodist

---

24. The second stanza of Charles Wesley's hymn "All Things Are Possible to Him," in *CHPCM*, 563–64.

25. Wesley, "To John Fletcher," January 15, 1773, in *The Letters of John Wesley*, 6:10–12.

26. See Forsaith, "Wesley's Designated Successor."

and in some ways not friendly to Methodism—but this is what he said about John Fletcher: "No age or country has ever produced a man of more fervid piety or more perfect charity. No church has ever possessed a more apostolic minister. Fletcher, in any communion, would have been a saint."[27] He would indeed. Listen to what Canon Overton said about him: "He was not a Christian: he was Christlike."[28] Do you remember what Voltaire said? Do you? Do you remember Voltaire discussing it once, I think it was with Boswell, though Boswell does not mention it in his journal.[29] In those long conversations they had on religion, and at times sneered about our faith, and Boswell said, "Voltaire, did you ever meet anybody like Jesus Christ?" Voltaire stopped in his stride and all the heat went out of him and he said, "I once met Fletcher of Madeley." Oh, if I tell you that his wife said she'd lived with an angel[30] and that when John Wesley came to preach his sermon, his funeral sermon, he opened the book and put the text, "Behold the Perfect Man" [Ps 37:37][31]—John Wesley, with his standards, gives out that text, "Behold the Perfect Man"—you'll begin to sense the quality of life our people had. Jealous, censorious, critical, pushing for place? No, no! No, no! They had, they had received the Holy Spirit, and Christ in them was formed afresh.

But my friends it isn't on that kind of testimony that I want to rely now because people exaggerate sometimes. Now listen, having read on sanctity for twenty-five years,[32] I would rather, I would rather pick up a few ordinary

27. Tyerman, *Wesley's Designated Successor*, v–vi.

28. Abbey and Overton, *English Church in the Eighteenth Century*, 343.

29. Albert Outler makes a more likely suggestion that the original source of this story was John Fletcher's brother-in-law, Monsieur de Bottons, who was also an intimate friend of Voltaire. Whaling, ed., *John and Charles Wesley: Selected Prayers, Hymns, Journal Notes, Sermons, Letters and Treaties*, 40.

30. Her actual words at his funeral were, "Three years, nine months, and two days, I have possessed my *heavenly-minded husband* . . ." In Tyerman, *Wesley's Designated Successor*, 565.

31. Fletcher's actual funeral sermon was preached by the Rev. Thomas Hatton from a neighbouring parish. Wesley's tribute sermon of October 24, 1785 was entitled "On the Death of Rev. Mr. John Fletcher" (*BE*, 3:609–29), with the full biblical text being, "Mark the perfect man, and behold the upright: For the end of that man is peace" (Ps 37:37).

32. Sangster's first published article dedicated specifically to sanctity was "Is Christ Only a Partial Saviour?" *Methodist Recorder*, April 8, 1937, 15. Though his real engagement with the Methodist doctrine of sanctification came as a consequence of his personal crisis of 1930 and an experience of "assurance" mediated through the Oxford Group movement, through which he attributes rediscovering the witness of the Spirit and links this specifically to John Wesley's Sermon 10, "The Witness of the Spirit." W. E. Sangster, "Search for Certainty," *Methodist Recorder*, September 14, 1933, 7. For further discussion of this early engagement of Sangster with his Methodist inheritance, see Cheatle, *W. E. Sangster – Herald of Holiness*, 38–45.

questions that we might use—we plain people—as tests of our progress and see how, how Fletcher stands up to these. And if you want day-to-day and ordinary tests of this quality of life I'll take things as plain and down to earth as this. I would ask if such a man, "Has he mastery over the love of money? Can he suffer and keep sweet? Is worldly ambition dead in him? Can he engage in controversy and remain loving?" They'll do. I could give a dozen more—they'll do! Let's look at each of them in turn and let's see how Fletcher passes all the tests.

Has he mastery over the love of money? Oh, plenty of us are generous with our surplus. Plenty of use are capable of minor generosities out of major resources. This man, this man gave till it hurt. He had little enough, and God alone knows how he lived on the little he kept for himself. He gave not of his surplus but of his substance. And when he died, though the rapture of heaven was in full view, he died saying, "My poor, my poor, oh, who will look after my poor?"[33] Has the Holy Spirit mastered the love of money in you? Our pockets are the last part of us to be converted. In these days when it is still rare for people to give a tenth—to give a tenth, the old tithe store—has the Holy Spirit mastered the love of money in us, in the churches? Has he? And are we worthy then to call ourselves the spiritual sons and daughters of this holy man?

Can he suffer and keep sweet? There are lots of people who appear to be on the way to sanctity but they disintegrate in suffering. I had a man in my church once who I thought was on the way to sanctity and then fell ill. And he was taken to the hospital. And I thought, "It will be a privilege for the nurses to nurse him. Everybody in the ward will be blessed by him when he's gets better. Now you'll see that lovely life irradiate the hospital." He didn't. He didn't. He grew peevish in suffering. He was complaining. He made hard tasks harder still by his whining. I was mistaken. He couldn't pass that test. He couldn't suffer and keep sweet. Fletcher could. He suffered terribly. Five years he was off work at one period. He came back seraphic, his soul aflame, nearer to God than ever. His soul battled on the strong meat of suffering. He learned to love his Lord's cross more in bearing his own. Could you suffer and keep sweet?

Or this, or this question: Is worldly ambition dead in him? That's a question I put to myself when candidates for sanctity are put forward. And one of the questions, "Is worldly ambition dead in him?"; it was in Fletcher. Oh, you must have heard the story of how once he nearly had great preferment. Dr. Eugene Smith, the other morning, in that most able speech he gave us, reminded those you who do not know England that the Anglican Church is

---

33. Mrs. Fletcher's paper read at her husband's funeral by the Rev. Hatton, in Tyerman, *Wesley's Designated Successor*, 565.

an established church.[34] It's tied to the state and preferment can come from the state. And prime ministers can give you a push up in the church. John Fletcher, like John Wesley, was a leader of the Methodists and in Anglican orders too. And one day he made a speech that helped the government of the day very much. He didn't make the speech to help them; he made the speech because he thought it was true. But it did help them. And they were grateful. And the lord chancellor said, "Who is this Fletcher of Madeley? They tell me he's a parson." And they told him, "Oh yes, he's a friend and helper of John Wesley. He's vicar of Madeley in Shropshire." "Oh," he said, "is he in the establishment? We could do something for him." So, from Whitehall a messenger was dispatched to the rectory, the rustic rectory at Madeley, which I know so well. And when he arrived the saint didn't know why he'd come. "A gentleman come all the way from London to see me, how kind. Oh, do come in. Do come in." And he started dropping hints, this gentleman. But you know saints are slower than other people in some ways. They are. I mean, look, their eye isn't sharp with self-seeking, and their ear isn't attuned to knowing how they can get something for themselves. He didn't pick up the hint. The gentleman kept talking about, "Er, wouldn't he, er, like to be nearer London?" Madeley was a quiet place. In the end the hints were bouncing on the rectory floor, and he still didn't know. He had to be crude at the last, quite crude. He had to say, "Look Mr. Fletcher, do you want anything? Do you? Big people are behind this. Would you like a canonry? Would you like to be a dean? What about a bishopric, Mr. Fletcher?" And then he understood. And he said, "Oh, how kind, how very kind. But I don't want anything except more grace."[35]

There's your saint! God knows when he has his man then. It's spreads out before him: "There you are, the prizes of the world and you can have them in the church. We'll top it up with a halo. You can be a bishop. Go on!" And he says, "I don't want anything but more grace."

My dear friends, I don't know really whether it's true, but I'm told that there are some branches of Methodism where fellows "put up" for the bishopric. "Run for it" is the term, I'm told. They run for it. Put themselves forward and say, "Vote for me!" Oh, have you carried the hustings into the

---

34. Eugene L. Smith (1920–86), American United Methodist minister, a true ecumenist. Smith directed the foreign missions of the United Methodist Church for sixteen years before serving as the executive secretary of the United States Conference of the World Conference of Churches from 1964 to 1973. *New York Times*, February 25, 1986; and "Eugene L. Smith Sr." His address at the conference, entitled "New United Churches and Suggested Plans of Union," was delivered at 9:30 a.m. on Friday September 7, 1956. Clark and Perkins, eds., *Proceedings*, 24.

35. Wesley, *Life and Death of the Rev. John Fletcher Vicar of Madeley*, cited in Tyerman, *Wesley's Designated Successor*, 353.

sanctuary? Have you done that? Then listen. One of your spiritual forebears was this John Fletcher. He was called to be a saint—and became one, by the same agency that you could; by the energies of the Holy Ghost. And when, and when they would press preferment upon him, he said, "But I want nothing except more grace."

Can you engage in controversy and remain loving? Some of you will say, "Oh, but saints don't join in controversy, do they?" *Don't* they? *Don't* they? Don't you mistake the character of a saint. I said just now, "He grasps his faith with its firm dogmatic heart." It isn't nebulous sentiment with him. He hasn't any of this nonsense about, "It doesn't matter what you believe so long as you behave aright." He knows the stupidity of that. He holds the faith. And when it's in danger he defends it. The only thing is this: he does it with love, with melting love, like John Fletcher did. All his major writings were controversial works, the whole lot of them.[36] He was engaged in the most odius theological quarrel that disturbed the eighteenth century. He was! He went through the fire! There isn't a smell of burning on him! Not a smell. He came out of that dirty battle unstained, which is more than can be said of Augustus Toplady,[37] or even William Law, or even George Whitefield, or even John Wesley.[38] Henry Venn, one man who withstood him in the heat of their controversy, had him in his home afterwards; wouldn't let him go, kept him for six weeks, and then said, "It was like having an angel in the house."[39]

Well we're not out of religious controversy yet. I understand that there are people in America who are calling the World Council of Churches "that great Babylonish whore."[40] I was preaching in one part of your great country recently and I was told of one man who engaged in controversy—bitter and denunciatory. I couldn't believe his quoted words and I said to my informant, "Please, please, you will tell me next he doesn't preach Christ." "Oh," he said, "he preaches Christ like the devil."

My dear friends, see this holy man; again I'm pleading with you not to regard him as rare. He was rare maybe in his mental power, a little distinguished in the notice that came to him, but in the quality of life I am expounding he was not rare. In all walks of life, there were thousands of them. God didn't give it in response to intellect; he gave it in response to faith. In all walks

---

36. Streiff, *Reluctant Saint*; Forsaith, *John Fletcher*.

37. Maycock, "Fletcher-Toplady Controversy."

38. Forsaith, ed., *Unexampled Labours: Letters of the Rev. John Fletcher*.

39. A free interpretation of Henry Venn's words about Fletcher in two letters, in Tyerman, *Wesley's Designated Successor*, 394, 570.

40. A reference to Rev 17 and 18 (e.g., 17:1, 5).

of life—the miner, the ploughman, the housewife—they opened themselves to it. Believed for it! And God came in and did it for them.

Well, our conference, I say, draws to its end. Many of you have said in my hearing, "We want a firmer theology. We do." Why not begin with this? It's our own treasure, the neglected treasure. You've sometimes left it to the cranks, who misunderstood it, and unconsciously caricatured it, some of them.[41] Oh, I beg you, capture again the Methodist doctrine of holiness. See how it panels in to sanctity in every communion, but see the distinctive note we have here, and you'll never think that our theology is the same theology of the other Reformed communions. We have a distinctive note here. And if they don't know it in those other communions you ought to tell them, but it would be still more helpful to illustrate it to them.

It has been said again and again in this conference, "We're neglecting the doctrine of the Holy Spirit." So we are. Start here. One of the first tasks of the Holy Spirit is to come in response to faith into the heart of the believer and make him holy. Why not? Some of you have been saying in my presence, "We seem to have lost power with the poorer people and become a middle-class church." This is the way to power. The world cannot long resist a holy church. We're all wanting the answer to race problems. We all know, it's here. It's here. Have this and you'll have them. This isn't just personal piety. You must know that when you think of the life of Wesley and all the wonderful social service that came to pass, this spreads out. The people keen on social service without this, they'll never get the end they're seeking. It's an occupation for saints. Well, there it is. I'm saying this about our forebears:

> They saw the goal!
> We do not so clearly see the goal.
>
> They knew the way!
> We do not so plainly know the way.
>
> They reached the heights!
> We stumble in the foothills.
>
> May God have mercy on us all.

---

41. Sangster rejected the narrow, often world-denying, and in some ways triumphalist interpretation of John Wesley's theology by the theologians and churches of the Holiness Movement within and beyond Methodism, engaging in debate with them in publications and correspondence. For a detailed discussion, see Cheatle, *W. E. Sangster – Herald of Holiness*, 114–16, 141, 145–47.

Let us pray:

O God, our Father, set aside any word if it is not thy word.

But if indeed, if this is thy word to us,

O God, help us to translate it into life.

We have so much our forebears did not have.

Have we lost something precious that they possessed?

Art thou still willing to work this change our human hearts?

Does faith open us to the mighty energies of God?

Will the Holy Spirit be resident in our unworthy souls?

O God, as we sing our last hymn and make it a prayer.

Answer that prayer in all our lives.

For Jesu's sake,

Amen.

Bibliography

Abbey, Charles J., John H. Overton. *The English Church in the Eighteenth Century*. New ed. London: Longmans, Green, 1887.

Ambler, Rex. "The Light Within—Then and Now." A talk to the Quaker Universalist Conference, Woodbrooke, March 2010.

Augustine. *Confessions*. Edited by R. S. Pine-Coffin. London: Penguin, 2002.

Baker, Anne Pimlott. "Boycott, Charles Cunningham (1832–1897)." *Oxford Dictionary of National Biography*. Oxford: Oxford University Press, 2004. http://www.oxforddnb.com/view/article/3100.

Baker, Frank, *John Wesley and the Church of England*, 2nd ed. London: Epworth, 2000.

Barclay, William, *Christ in You: A Study in Paul's Theology and Ethics*. Boston: University Press, 1999.

Bax, Ernest Belfort, *The Rise and Fall of the Anabaptists*. London: Swan Sonnenschein, 1901.

Bebbington, David. "Methodist Spirituality, 1800–1950." http://www.methodistheritage.org.uk/missionary-history-bebbington-spirituality-2004.pdf.

Bennett, Clinton. "Martyn, Henry." In *Biographical Dictionary of Christian Missions*, edited by Gerald H. Anderson, 438–39. New York: Macmillan Reference, 1998.

Berry, Sidney, ed. *The Little Book of Sermons*. [London]: Sunday Times, 1959.

Beswick, Frank. "Two-Ocean Passenger: Sydney to London Via Pacific and Atlantic." *Flight*, January 29, 1954, 121.

Birkett, D. J. "Slessor, Mary Mitchell (1848–1915)." *Oxford Dictionary of National Biography*. Oxford: Oxford University Press, 2004. http://www.oxforddnb.com/view/article/37973.

Bliss, Michael. "Banting, Sir Frederick Grant (1891–1941)." *Oxford Dictionary of National Biography*. Oxford: Oxford University Press, 2004. http://www.oxforddnb.com/view/article/30576.

Booth, William. *In Darkest England and the Way Out*. London: International Headquarters of the Salvation Army, 1890.

Brabazon, James. *Albert Schweitzer: A Biography*. 2nd ed. Syracuse, NY: Syracuse University Press, 2000.

Bradley, James, and Jay Lamar, eds. *Charles Darwin: A Celebration of His Life and Legacy*. Montgomery, AL: New South, 2013.

Brake, George Thomson. *Policy and Politics in British Methodism 1932–82*. London: Edsall, 1984.

Britton, Andrew. *RMS Elizabeth*. Stroud: History Press, 2013.

Brockway, Fenner. *Bermondsey Story: The Life of Alfred Salter.* London: Allen and Unwin, 1949.

Brown, Judith M. "Gandhi, Mohandas Karamchand [Mahatma Gandhi] (1869–1948)." *Oxford Dictionary of National Biography.* Oxford: Oxford University Press, 2004. http://www.oxforddnb.com/view/article/33318.

Brown, Derek. "1956: Suez and the End of Empire." *Guardian,* March 14, 2001. https://www.theguardian.com/politics/2001/mar/14/past.education1.

Bunting, Joyce. "Salisbury, Francis Owen (1874–1962), Britain's Painter Laureate." http://www.harpenden-history.org.uk/page_id__413.aspx.

Burton, Harold. *The Life of St. Francis de Sales.* Vol. 1. London: Burns, Oats and Washbourne, 1925.

Cadbury, Deborah. *Seven Wonders of the Industrial World.* London and New York: Fourth Estate, 2003.

Campbell, John. "Smith, Frederick Edwin, First Earl of Birkenhead (1872–1930)." *Oxford Dictionary of National Biography.* Oxford: Oxford University Press, 2004. http://www.oxforddnb.com/view/article/36137.

Carnall, Geoffrey. "Southey, Robert (1774–1843)." *Oxford Dictionary of National Biography.* Oxford: Oxford University Press, 2004. http://www.oxforddnb.com/view/article/26056.

Carnegie, Dale. *How to Win Friends and Influence People.* New York: Simon and Schuster, 1936.

Carré, E. G., ed. *Praying Hyde: The Apostle of Prayer.* Alachua, FL: Bridge-Logos, 1982.

Casey, T. F. "Vianney, Jean Baptiste Marie, St." In *New Catholic Encyclopedia,* edited by Berard L. Marthaler, 14:469–70. 2nd ed. Washington, DC: Thomson/Gale, 2003,

Castle, W. B. "The Gordon Wilson Lecture: A Century of Curiosity About Pernicious Anemia." *Transactions of the American Clinical Climatological Association* 73 (1962) 54–80.

Cheatle, Andrew J. "Reflections on the Creation of a Research Archive on one of the Mid-Twentieth Century's Most Renowned Religious Figures." *Fieldwork in Religion,* November 2013.

————. *W. E. Sangster - Herald of Holiness: A Critical Analysis of the Doctrines of Sanctification and Perfection in the Thought of W. E. Sangster.* Milton Keynes: Paternoster, 2011.

————. *William Sangster: Heir of John Wesley?* Ilkeston: Moorleys, 2013.

"Chronological List of Presidents, First Ladies, and Vice Presidents of the United States." Library of Congress, Prints and Photographs Division, 20540-4730. https://www.loc.gov/rr/print/list/057_chron.html.

Clark, Elmer T., and E. Benson Perkins, eds. *Proceedings of the Ninth World Methodist Conference,* Nashville: Methodist Publishing, 1957

Coué, Émile. *Self-Mastery Through Conscious Autosuggestion.* Reprint of 1926 ed. London: Allen and Unwin, 1957.

Cross, F. L., and E. A. Livingstone, eds. *Oxford Dictionary of the Christian Church.* Oxford: University Press, 2005.

Cumbers, Frank H. *Richmond College 1843–1943.* London: Epworth, 1944.

Darwin, Francis, ed. *The Life and Letters of Charles Darwin.* Vol. 1. Project Gutenberg ebook, 1999. http://www.gutenberg.org/files/2087/2087-h/2087-h.htm.

David, Saul. *The Homicidal Earl: The Life of Lord Cardigan.* London: Little, Brown, 1997.

Davis, Mary. "An Historical Introduction to the Campaign for Equal Pay." At Trade Union Congress. http://www.unionhistory.info/equalpay/roaddisplay.php?irn=820.

Davies, Horton. *The Varieties of English Preaching 1900–1960*. London: SCM, 1963.

De Haan, Francisca. "Fry, Elizabeth (1780–1845)." *Oxford Dictionary of National Biography*. Oxford: Oxford University Press, 2004. http://www.oxforddnb.com/view/article/10208.

Deissmann, Adolf Gustav. *Die Neutestamentliche Formel, In Christo Jesu*. Marburg: Elwert, 1892.

Desmond, Adrian, James Moore, and Janet Browne. "Darwin, Charles Robert (1809–1882)." *Oxford Dictionary of National Biography*. Oxford: Oxford University Press, 2004. http://www.oxforddnb.com/view/article/7176.

Dorr, Luther M. "A Critique of the Preaching of William Edwin Robert Sangster." PhD diss., New Orleans Baptist Theological Seminary, 1968.

Duncan, Stewart. "Thomas Hobbes." *Stanford Encyclopedia of Philosophy*, edited by Edward N. Zalta. Summer 2017 ed. https://plato.stanford.edu/archives/sum2017/entries/hobbes/.

Emerson, Ralph Waldo. "Social Aims." In *The Complete Works of Ralph Waldo Emerson*. http://www.rwe.org/social-aims/.

"Eugene L. Smith Sr." *York Daily Record & York Dispatch*, February 12, 2006. http://www.legacy.com/obituaries/york/obituary.aspx?n=eugene-l-smith&pid=16669923&fhid=4789.

Fisher, Geoffrey. "Archbishop Fisher's Cambridge Sermon, 1946." In R.P. Findall, *The Church of England 1815–1948*, London: SPCK, 1972.

"Fletcher, John." *Encyclopedia Britannica*, 10:498. 11th ed.

Foote, Gaston, ed. *Communion Meditations*. New York: Abingdon-Cokesbury, 1951.

Forsaith, Peter S. "Fletcher, John William (1729–1785)." *Dictionary of Methodism in Britain and Ireland*. http://www.wesleyhistoricalsociety.org.uk/dmbi/index.php?do=app.entry&id=205.

———. *John Fletcher*. Peterborough: Epworth, 1994.

———. *Unexampled Labours: Letters of the Rev. John Fletcher to leaders in the Evangelical Revival*. Peterborough: Epworth, 2008.

———. "Wesley's Designated Successor." *Proceedings of the Wesley Historical Society* 42/3 (1979) 69–74.

Ghéon, Henri. *The Secret of the Curé D'Ars*. London: Sheed and Ward, 1936.

Gilbert, R. E. "Eisenhower's 1955 Heart Attack: Medical Treatment, Political Effects, and the 'Behind The Scenes' Leadership Style." *Journal of the Association of Politics and the Life Sciences* 27/1 (2008) 2–21.

Greet, Kenneth G. "Perkins, Ernest Benson." *Dictionary of Methodism in Britain and Ireland*. http://www.wesleyhistoricalsociety.org.uk/dmbi/index.php?do=app.entry&id=2175.

Grimwood, Thomas. "The Limits of Misogyny: Schopenhauer on, 'Women.'" *Kritike* 2/2 (2010) 131–45.

Hanninen, O., M. Farago, and E. Monos. "Ignaz Philipp Semmelweis: The Prophet of Bacteriology." *Infection Control* 4 (1983) 367–70.

Hattersley, Roy. *Blood & Fire: William and Catherine Booth and the Salvation Army*. London: Little, Brown, 1999.

Hauser, Benjamin Gayelord. *Look Younger, Live Longer*. New York: Farrar, Straus, 1950.

Hildebrandt, Franz, and Oliver A. Beckerlegge, eds. *A Collection of Hymns for the Use of the People Called Methodist.* Vol. 7 of *The Works of John Wesley*, Bicentennial Edition. Nashville: Abingdon, 1983.

Hobbes, Thomas. *Of Man, Being the First Part of Leviathan.* Harvard Classics. New York: P. F. Collier and Son, 1909–14. http://www.bartleby.com/34/5/13.html.

Holmes, Oliver, *Ralph Waldo Emerson: Biography.* Luxembourg: Creative English Publishing, 2013.

Howell, David. "Salter, Alfred (1873–1945)." *Oxford Dictionary of National Biography.* Oxford: Oxford University Press, 2004. http://www.oxforddnb.com/view/article/50376.

Jackson, Clare. "Scougal, Henry (1650–1678)" *Oxford Dictionary of National Biography.* Oxford: Oxford University Press, 2004. http://www.oxforddnb.com/view/article/24941.

James, Maynard. "Dr Sangster's New Book." *The Flame*, May–June 1943, 2, 27.

Jones, John. "Farmer, John (1835–1901)." *Oxford Dictionary of National Biography.* Oxford: Oxford University Press, 2004. http://www.oxforddnb.com/view/article/33081.

Jones, R. V. "Watt, Sir Robert Alexander Watson (1892–1973)." *Oxford Dictionary of National Biography.* Oxford: Oxford University Press, 2004. http://www.oxforddnb.com/view/article/31811.

Jørgensen, Johannes. *Saint Francis of Assisi.* London: Longmans, Green, 1912.

"Kanton Atoll." *Encyclopedia Britannica.* http://library.eb.co.uk/levels/adult/article/44617.

Ker, Ian. *John Henry Newman: A Biography.* Oxford: Oxford University Press, 1988.

Larsen, David L. "William E. Sangster: In the Wake of the Wesleys." *Preaching*, May 3, 2008, 8.

Law, William. *The Spirit of Prayer.* 1758. https://www.ccel.org/ccel/law/prayer/files/prayer.html.

Lawton, George. "John Fletcher's Incumbency at Madeley." *London Quarterly and Holborn Review*, October 1956, 281–87.

———. "Madeley in the Eighteenth Century." *London Quarterly and Holborn Review*, April 1956, 142–48.

Lazell, David. *Gypsy from the Forest: A New Biography of the International Evangelist Gypsy Smith (1860–1947).* Darlington: Evangelical, 2004.

Leaming, Barbara. *If This Was Happiness: A Biography of Rita Hayworth.* London: Penguin, 1989.

Leibman, Joshua Loth. *Peace of Mind.* New York: Simon and Schuster, 1946.

Levick, Barbara. "Pliny in Bithynia and What Followed." *Greece and Rome* 26/2 (1979) 119–31.

Lewis, Peter B. *Arthur Schopenhauer.* London: Reaktion, 2013.

Lloyd-Jones, Martin. *Preaching and Preachers.* London: Hodder and Stoughton, 1971.

Lord, Townley F., ed. *Harvest Sermons.* London: Independent, 1957.

Loughlin-Chow, Clare M. "Bowdler, Thomas (1754–1825)." *Oxford Dictionary of National Biography.* Oxford: Oxford University Press, 2004. http://www.oxforddnb.com/view/article/3032.

Luff, William G. *The Story of the Ocean City Tabernacle.* Ocean City, NJ: Luff/QPS, 1995.

Macpherson, Ian, ed. *Sermon Outlines from Sermon Masters.* New York: Abingdon, 1960.

———. *Sermon Outlines from Sermon Masters, Old Testament.* New York: Abingdon, 1962.

Marthaler, Berard L., ed. "Vianney, Jean Baptiste Marie, St." In *New Catholic Encyclopedia*, edited by Berard L. Marthaler, 14:469–70. 2nd ed. Washington, DC: Thomson/Gale, 2003.

Matthew, H. C. G. "Nicoll, Sir William Robertson (1851–1923)." *Oxford Dictionary of National Biography*. Oxford: Oxford University Press, 2004. http://www.oxforddnb.com/view/article/35236.

Maycock, J. "The Fletcher-Toplady Controversy." *London Quarterly and Holborn Review*, July 1966, 227–235.

McIntyre, N. "Alexander Fleming (1881–1955)." *Journal of Medical Biography*, November 15, 2007, 234.

Morson, Geoffrey V. "Macintosh, Charles (1766–1843)", *Oxford Dictionary of National Biography*. Oxford: Oxford University Press, 2004. http://www.oxforddnb.com/view/article/17541.

Murray, Iain. *Wesley and the Men Who Followed*. Edinburgh: Banner of Truth, 2003.

Nickalls, John, ed. *The Journal of George Fox*. Cambridge: Cambridge University Press, 1952.

Noble, Charles "Salisbury, Francis Owen (1874–1962)." *Oxford Dictionary of National Biography*. Oxford: Oxford University Press, 2004. http://www.oxforddnb.com/view/article/35912.

Noren, Carol M. "The Ten Greatest Preachers of the Twentieth Century." *Preaching.com*. https://www.preaching.com/articles/the-ten-greatest-preachers-of-the-twentieth-century/.

Padwick, Constance E. *Henry Martyn: Confessor of the Faith*. London: Inter-Varsity, 1922

Parkes, William, "Watchnight, Covenant Service and Love-Feast in Early British Methodism." *Wesleyan Theological Journal* 32/2 (1997).

Perkins, Ernest Benson, and Albert Hearn. *The Methodist Church Builds Again*. London Epworth, 1946.

Quiller-Couch, Arthur. *Hetty Wesley*. London: Dent and Sons, 1908.

Rackemann, F. M. *The Inquistive Physician: The Life and Times of George Richard Minot* Cambridge, MA: Harvard University Press, 1956.

Radice, William. "Tagore, Rabindranath (1861–1941)." *Oxford Dictionary of National Biography*. Oxford: Oxford University Press, 2004. http://www.oxforddnb.com/view/article/36404.

Railton, George Scott. *The Authoritative Life of William Booth*. Teddington: Echo Library, 2007.

Randall, Ian M. *Evangelical Experiences*. Carlisle: Paternoster, 1999.

Ratter, Magnus. *Albert Schweitzer: A Biography*. London: Lindsey, 1949.

Reed, John. *Catherine Booth: Laying the Theological Foundations of a Radical Movement*. Eugene, OR: Pickwick, 2013.

Roberts, A. D. "Livingstone, David (1813–1873)." *Oxford Dictionary of National Biography*. Oxford: Oxford University Press, 2004. http://www.oxforddnb.com/view/article/16803.

Roberts, Helen M. *Champion of the Silent Billion: The Story of Frank C. Laubach, Apostle of Literacy*. St. Paul, MN: Macelester Park, 1961.

Rodger, N. A. M. "Montagu, John, Fourth Earl of Sandwich (1718–1792)." *Oxford Dictionary of National Biography*. Oxford: Oxford University Press, 2004. http://www.oxforddnb.com/view/article/19026.

Rolfe, John C., trans. *Ammianus Marcellinus*. LCL. Cambridge, MA: Harvard University Press, 1935.

Salomons, W., B. L. Bayne, E. K. Duursma, and U. Förstner, eds. "North Sea." *Pollution of the North Sea: An Assessment*. Berlin: Springer, 1988.

"Sandwich Celebrates 250th Anniversary of the Sandwich." BBC, May 12, 2012. http://www.bbc.co.uk/news/uk-england-kent-18010424.

Sangster, Paul. *Doctor Sangster*. London: Epworth, 1962.

Sangster, W. E. *The Approach to Preaching*. London: Epworth, 1951.

———. *Are You Superstitious?* Stirling: n.p., 1943.

———. *A Check-Up for Our Church*. Westminster Pamphlet 2. London: Epworth, 1956.

———. *The Craft of Sermon Construction*. London: Epworth, 1949.

———. *The Craft of Sermon Illustration*. London: Epworth, 1946.

———. *The Craft of the Sermon*. London: Epworth, 1954.

———. *Doctrinal Preaching: Its Neglect and Recovery*. Birmingham: Berean, 1953.

———. *Give God a Chance*. London: Epworth, 1959.

———. *God Does Guide Us*. London: Hodder and Stoughton, 1934.

———. "God's Greatest Gift." In *Sermons I Should Like to Have Preached*, edited by Ian Macpherson, 78–85. New York: Revell, 1964.

———. *The Great Mystery of the Afterlife*. London: Hodder and Stoughton, 1957.

———. *The Greatest of These . . .* Westminster Pamphlet 12. London: Epworth, 1959.

———. "The Heavenly Vision." In *Let Us Worship*, edited by David N. Francis, 58–63. London: Epworth, 1962.

———. *He Is Able*. London: Hodder and Stoughton, 1936.

———. *Holiness*. Pharos Papers 5. London: Epworth, 1950.

———. *How Much Are You Saved?* Westminster Pamphlet 11. London: Epworth, 1959.

———. "How to Be Saved." In *Evangelical Sermons of Our Day*, edited by Andrew W. Blackwood, 300–306. New York: Harper, 1959.

———. *How to Form a Prayer Cell*. Westminster Pamphlet 10. London: Epworth, 1958.

———. *How to Live in Christ*. Westminster Pamphlet 8. London: Epworth, 1957.

———. *Let Me Commend*. London: Hodder and Stoughton, 1948.

———. *Methodism Can Be Born Again*. London: Hodder and Stoughton, 1938.

———. *Methodism: Her Unfinished Task*. London: Epworth, 1947.

———. *The Path to Perfection*. London: Hodder and Stoughton, 1943.

———. *Power in Preaching*. London: Epworth, 1958.

———. *Prayer*. London: Epworth, 1936.

———. *A Programme for Youth*. Westminster Pamphlet 9. London: Epworth, 1958.

———. *Providence*. London: Epworth, 1937.

———. *The Pure in Heart*. London: Epworth, 1954.

———. *Revival: The Need and the Way*. Westminster Pamphlet 7. London: Epworth, 1957.

———. "Richmond and Evangelism." In *Richmond College 1843–1943*, edited by Frank H. Cumbers, 25–26. London: Epworth, 1944.

———. *Sangster at Filey*. Croydon: New Mildway, 1961.

———. *The Secret of Radiant Life*. London: Hodder and Stoughton, 1957.

———. *A Spiritual Check-Up*. Westminster Pamphlet 1. London: Epworth, 1952.

———. "The Spiritual Meaning of Advent." *Special Day Sermons for Evangelicals*, edited by Andrew W. Blackwood, 50–59. Great Neck, NY: Channel, 1961.

———. *Teach Us to Pray*. London: Epworth, 1951.

———. *Ten Statesmen & Jesus Christ*. London: Hodder and Stoughton, 1941.

————. *These Things Abide*. London: Hodder and Stoughton, 1939.

————. *They Met at Calvary*. London: Epworth, 1956.

————. *Twelve Ways of Evangelism*. Westminster Pamphlet 3. London: Epworth, 1952.

————. *Twelve Ways of Service*. Westminster Pamphlet 4. London: Epworth, 1956.

————. *Westminster Sermons*. Vols. 1 and 2. London: Epworth, 1960, 1962.

————. *Why Jesus Never Wrote a Book*. London: Hodder and Stoughton, 1932.

————. *You Can Be a Millionaire*. Westminster Pamphlet 5. London: Epworth, 1957.

————. *You Can Be a Saint*. Westminster Pamphlet 6. London: Epworth, 1957.

Sangster, W. E., and Leslie Davison. *The Pattern of Prayer*. London: Epworth, 1962.

Schweitzer, Albert *The Quest of the Historical Jesus*. London: A & C Black, 1911.

Scotland, Nigel. *Squires in the Slums: Settlements and Missions in Late Victorian Britain* London: I. B. Tauris, 2007.

Server, Lee. *Ava Gardner: Love Is Nothing*. London: Bloomsbury, 2006.

Shipley, David. "Methodist Arminianism in the Theology of John Fletcher." PhD diss., Yale University, 1942.

Shorter, Edward. *How Everyone Became Depressed: The Rise and Fall of the Nervous Breakdown*. Oxford: Oxford University Press, 2013.

Smith, Frederick Edwin. *Hansard 4*, 153, March 12, 1906, 1014–23.

Snyder, C. Arnold. *Anabaptist History and Theology*. Kitchener, ON: Pandora, 1995.

Spoto, Daniel, *Marilyn Monroe: The Biography*. New ed. London: Arrow, 1994.

Stewart, Duncan. "Hobbes, Thomas." *Stanford Encyclopedia of Philosophy*, edited by Edward N. Zalta. Summer 2017 ed. http://plato.stanford.edu/entries/hobbes/.

Streiff, Patrick. *Reluctant Saint: a theological Biography of Fletcher of Madeley*. Peterborough: Epworth, 2001.

"Suez Crisis." *Encyclopedia Britannica*. https://www.britannica.com/event/Suez-Crisis.

Sweetman, John "Brudenell, James Thomas, Seventh earl of Cardigan (1797–1868)." *Oxford Dictionary of National Biography*. Oxford: Oxford University Press, 2004. http://www.oxforddnb.com/view/article/3765.

Tagore, Rabindranath. "Gitanjali Poem No. 50." https://archive.org/stream/ gitanjalisongoffootagouoft/gitanjalisongoffootagouoft_djvu.txt.

Teresa de Ávila. *Interior Castle*. Translated and edited by Allison E. Peers. Mineola, NY: Dover, 2007.

Thames Water. "End of an Era for the Sewage Sludge Boats." *PR Newswire* December 30, 1998. http://www.prnewswire.co.uk/news-releases/end-of-an-era-for-the-sewage-sludge-boats-156225755.html.

Travell, John C. *Doctor of Souls: Leslie D. Weatherhead 1893–1976*. Cambridge: James Clarke, 1999.

"The Late Bishop Brindle, D.S.O. A Military Funeral." *The Tablet*, July 8, 1916, 11.

Tucker, Austin B. *The Preacher as Storyteller*. Nashville: B & H, 2008.

Turberfield, Alan. *John Scott Lidgett, Archbishop of British Methodism?* Peterborough: Epworth, 2003.

Tyerman, Luke. *Wesley's Designated Successor*. London: Hodder & Stoughton, 1882.

Valentine, Simon Ross. *William Edwin Sangster*. Peterborough: Foundery, 1998.

Vickers, John A. "Smith, Rodney [called Gypsy Smith] (1860–1947), Evangelist." *Oxford Dictionary of National Biography*. Oxford: Oxford University Press, 2004. http:// www.oxforddnb.com/view/article/36155.

Wallace, William. *Life of Arthur Schopenhauer*. London: W. Scott, 1890.

Watson-Watt, Robert. *Three Steps to Victory*. Watford: Odhams, 1957.

Wesley, John. *The Life and Death of the Rev. John Fletcher Vicar of Madeley*. New York: Coper and Wilson, 1805.

———. *A Plain Account of Christian Perfection*. Unabridged ed. of 1872, authorized by the Wesleyan Conference Office. Kansas City, MO: Beacon Hill, 1966.

———. "To John Fletcher, 15 January 1773." In *The Letters of the Rev. John Wesley*, edited by John Telford. London: Epworth, 1931.

Whaling, Frank, ed. *John and Charles Wesley: Selected Prayers, Hymns, Journal Notes, Sermons, Letters and Treaties*. New York: Paulist, 1981.

Whitefield, George. *The Works of George Whitefield: Journals*. Banner of Truth Trust. Quinta, 2000.

Wilkinson, Alan. "Sheppard, Hugh Richard Lawrie (1880–1937)." *Oxford Dictionary of National Biography*. Oxford: Oxford University Press, 2004. http://www.oxforddnb.com/view/article/36061.

Worboys, Michael. "Fleming, Sir Alexander (1881–1955)." *Oxford Dictionary of National Biography*. Oxford: Oxford University Press, 2004. http://www.oxforddnb.com/view/article/33163.

Index of Names

Index of Subjects